The
Divine
Melody

Song of the Mystic Dove

*Compilation from the Writings of Bahá'u'lláh,
the Báb, 'Abdu'l-Bahá, Shoghi Effendi, and
the Universal House of Justice.*

Compiled by Lorraine Hétu Manifold

The Divine Melody: Song of the Mystic Dove

Source © Bahá'í International Community

Compiled by Lorraine Hétu Manifold

Cover design by Oscar Gomez

Publication © National Spiritual Assembly of the Bahá'ís of Australia Inc.
Published November 2022
All Rights Reserved

ISBN 978-1-925320-25-1
B.E. 180 edition

Distributed by
Bahá'í Distribution Services of Australia
173 Mona Vale Rd, Ingleside NSW, 2101

bds@bahai.org.au
www.bahaibooks.com.au

CONTENTS

Introduction   i

The Divine Melody   1

Melodies of Love & Praise   67

Melodies in the Mashriqu'l-Adhkár   117

Effort to Diffuse Divine Melodies   123

Introduction

Music can claim an exalted station in the Bahá'í Faith. Bahá'u'lláh says in the Kitáb-i-Aqdas (the Most Holy Book), "We, verily, have made music as a ladder for your souls, a means whereby they may be lifted up unto the realm on high..."[1] Like prayer, music is a powerful means to lift our spirits towards God. Instrumental music can touch us deeply and elevate our souls but when we set the Word of God to music and sing sacred songs, the combination is even more powerful. 'Abdu'l-Bahá elaborates:

> Music is like this glass which is perfectly pure and polished. It is precisely like this clear chalice before us. And the Teachings and Utterances of God are like the water. When the chalice is in the utmost state of purity, absolutely clear and polished, and the water is perfectly fresh, then it will confer life. Wherefore, the Teachings of God, whether they be Utterances in the form of homilies, or prayers and communes, when they are melodiously chanted will proved [sic] most impressive.[2]

Singing the Word of God can transform us, as Bahá'u'lláh affirms when He states that divinely-revealed words are "endowed with such potency as can instill new life into every human frame..."[3] Sacred songs based on the divine teachings can touch our souls and bring us closer to God. Anyone who has sung a prayer or the Word of God either alone or in a group will have felt the power that music has on their hearts

---

1   Bahá'u'lláh, *Kitáb-i-Aqdas*
2   *The Diary of Juliet Thompson*, pp. 81-82
3   Bahá'u'lláh, *Gleanings from the Writings of Bahá'u'lláh*

and souls. 'Abdu'l-Bahá refers to the Word of God as a melody that will change the world:

> ... know ye this: save for this song of God, no song will stir the world, and save for this nightingale-cry of truth from the Garden of God, no melody will lure away the heart. 'Whence cometh this Singer Who speaketh the Beloved's name?'[4]

In this passage 'Abdu'l-Bahá is perhaps also encouraging us to sing the Word of God as we work to transform the world. How uplifting that would be: singing to bring unity and peace to our neighbourhoods and communities all over the globe!

While there are already compilations on both Music[5] and the Arts,[6] numerous passages in the Writings refer to the Word of God as a melody. A search through the Bahá'í Writings reveals a multitude of passages where the Word of God is described as music being warbled by such creatures as the *Mystic Dove*, the *Dove of Truth* or of *Utterance*, the *Nightingale of Paradise* or of *Holiness*, the *Bird of Heaven*, of *Eternity*, or of *Holiness*, the *Spirit of God,* or sung by His *wondrous*, His *sublime*, His *all-compelling*, His *clear*, and *most eloquent* Voice.

In these passages, the Word of God itself is referred to in such terms as the *sweet Melodies of the spirit*, the *celestial Melody*, the *Melody of the Supreme Concourse*, the *soul-elevating harmony of heaven*, the *Melodies of thankful birds*.

---

4   'Abdu'l-Bahá, *Selections from the Writings of 'Abdu'l-Bahá*

5   Compilation on *Music*:
    bahai.org/library/authoritative-texts/compilations/music/

6   Compilation on *Arts*:
    bahai-library.com/pdf/compilations/arts.pdf
    Compilation on *The Importance of the Arts in Promoting the Faith*:
    bahai.org/library/authoritative-texts/compilations/importance-art/

It is interesting to consider how the concept of the Word of God as a divine melody could shape our Bahá'í communities going forward. Indeed, the future might be increasingly musically oriented as more Bahá'í-inspired music is created. Communities where group singing is not yet prevalent might discover a love of singing together. Shoghi Effendi reminds us that music is "an important feature of all Baha'i gatherings" and that the "Master Himself has emphasized its importance."[7] However, in order for people to feel comfortable singing as adults, musical education might need to start when we are young. 'Abdu'l-Bahá not only recommended that children study music, but said that music instruction is compulsory:

> It is incumbent upon each child to know something of music ... Likewise, it is necessary that the schools teach it in order that the souls and hearts of the pupils may become vivified and exhilarated and their lives be brightened with enjoyment.[8]

As a growing number of Bahá'í children learn music and go on to enter adulthood, our gatherings may naturally become more musical, with both children and adults playing instruments either alone or together. Likewise, singing may become a bigger part of our activities as musical abilities develop and we witness the power that music has to transform our inner and outer lives.

Further impetus to the global development of Bahá'í-inspired vocal music is given by the teaching that only live vocal music can be sung in the Houses of Worship:

---

7   Letter written on behalf of the Guardian to an individual believer, 17 March 1935, in *The Compilation of Compilations*, p. 80

8   'Abdu'l-Bahá, *The Promulgation of Universal Peace*

Music in the House of Worship is to be vocal only, whether by singers or a singer ...[and] all references to vocal music in the central Edifice imply the physical presence of the singers.[9]

As more local Houses of Worship are built, an exponential number of Bahá'í choirs will likely form, aligning with Shoghi Effendi's encouragement for choirs to sing in the Houses of Worship.[10] Singing in a House of Worship is an unforgettable experience that unites singers around one common goal, causes hearts to beat as one and lifts the spirits of both singers and audience up the rungs of a spiritual ladder towards the heavens.

The following compilation is by no means exhaustive, and as more Tablets are translated into English, other passages will undoubtedly emerge on this topic. The selection presented here includes Writings from the Bahá'í Faith that relate to the concept of the Divine Melody as well as passages that encourage us to sing this Divine Melody. Passages that refer more generally to music or the arts can be found in the compilations on Music and on the Arts published by the Research Department of the Universal House of Justice (see footnotes 5 and 6) and are not included here.

The first chapter focusses on Baha'i Writings in which the Word of God is referred to as a Divine Melody. This is followed by a selection of prayers to help us recognise or hearken to the Word of God. In the second chapter, the passages focus on how we can sing or impart the divine melodies. The third chapter presents a short series of quotes on the topic of singing the Divine Melodies in the Mashriqu'l-Adhkár. Finally, a brief

---

9   From a letter written by the Universal House of Justice to the National Spiritual Assembly of the United States, 13 March 1964

10   "Shoghi Effendi would urge that choir singing by men, women and children be encouraged in the Auditorium [of the Temple]." From a letter written on behalf of Shoghi Effendi to the National Spiritual Assembly of the United States and Canada, 2 April 1931

chapter is included on the concept of 'focus' as a virtue which is required in order both to spread the divine melodies and to sing them.

Understanding the Word of God as a Divine Melody can perhaps shed further light on the invitation of the International Teaching Centre to Bahá'í communities all over the world, to increase our use of the arts in all our endeavours:

> As with all other aspects of the expansion and consolidation work, the requirements of the time call on us to be more systematic in the use of the arts. They should not be considered simply an embellishment to our programs or an afterthought in our planning. Rather they must become an integral part of our teaching plans and community life. The arts have a vital role to play in the process of entry by troops. [11]

It is my hope that this compilation will encourage each one of us to hearken to the Divine Melodies and inspire us to sing God's praise and utilise the arts as we strive to, as Bahá'u'lláh proclaims, "promote the well-being and harmony of all the kindreds of the earth." [12]

Lorraine Hétu Manifold

---

11 From a letter written by the International Teaching Centre to the Continental Board of Counsellors, 5 November, 2001

12 Bahá'u'lláh, *Tablets of Bahá'u'lláh Revealed after the Kitáb-i-Aqdas*: "The source of crafts, sciences and arts is the power of reflection. Make ye every effort that out of this ideal mine there may gleam forth such pearls of wisdom and utterance as will promote the well-being and harmony of all the kindreds of the earth."

Note: Many of the quotes from the Bahá'í Writings were written in Persian or Arabic, where there is no masculine or feminine. While the English translation often uses the masculine pronouns, it is to be understood in the generic sense: 'man', 'he', 'his' are applicable to both women and men.

THE DIVINE MELODY

From the Writings of Bahá'u'lláh

Blessed the man who, assured of My Word, hath arisen from among the dead to celebrate My praise. Blessed is he that hath been enraptured by My wondrous melodies and hath rent the veils asunder through the potency of My might. Blessed is he who hath remained faithful to My Covenant, and whom the things of the world have not kept back from attaining My Court of holiness. Blessed is the man who hath detached himself from all else but Me, hath soared in the atmosphere of My love, hath gained admittance into My Kingdom, gazed upon My realms of glory, quaffed the living waters of My bounty, hath drunk his fill from the heavenly river of My loving providence, acquainted himself with My Cause, apprehended that which I concealed within the treasury of My Words, and hath shone forth from the horizon of divine knowledge engaged in My praise and glorification. Verily, he is of Me. Upon him rest My mercy, My loving-kindness, My bounty and My glory.

Tablets of Bahá'u'lláh Revealed After the Kitáb-i-Aqdas

Thus hath the Nightingale sung with sweet melody upon the celestial bough, in praise of its Lord, the All-Merciful. Well is it with them that hearken.

Kitáb-i-Aqdas

By the righteousness of God! But for the anthem of praise voiced by Him Who heralded the divine Revelation, this Wronged One would never have breathed a word which might have struck terror into the hearts of the ignorant and caused them to perish.

Tablets of Bahá'u'lláh Revealed After the Kitáb-i-Aqdas

O MY Name! Yield thou praise unto God for having graciously chosen thee to be a shower of bounty for that which We have sown in the pure and blessed soil and enabled thee to serve as a springtime of tender mercy for the wondrous and sublime trees We have planted. Indeed so great is this favour that of all created things in the world of existence, none can ever hope to rival it. We have moreover given thee to drink the choice wine of utterance from the chalice of the heavenly bestowals of thy merciful Lord, which is none other than this Tongue of holiness—a Tongue that, as soon as it was unloosed, quickened the entire creation, set in motion all beings and caused the Nightingale to pour forth its melodies. This is the Fountain of living water for all that dwell in the realm of being.

Tablets of Bahá'u'lláh Revealed After the Kitáb-i-Aqdas

O My Name! Suffer all created things to quaff once again from this chalice which hath caused the seas to rise. Kindle then in the hearts the blazing fire which this crimson Tree hath ignited, that they may arise to extol and magnify His Name amidst the adherents of all Faiths.

Numerous letters from thee have been presented before Our Throne. We have perused them as a token of grace on Our part, and for each name thou didst mention therein We have revealed that which will stir the minds of men and will cause the spirits to soar. Moreover We have repeatedly enabled thee to hearken unto the warblings of the birds of heaven and to incline thine ear to the songs of the nightingales pouring forth their melodies upon the branches. Thus was the Pen of God set in motion in thy remembrance that thou mightest admonish men through the power of this utterance which is divinely ordained to be the revealer of the signs of His glory. Blessed is the spot wherein the anthem of His praise is raised, and blessed the ear that hearkeneth unto that which hath been sent down from the heaven of the loving-kindness of thy Lord, the All-Merciful.

Tablets of Bahá'u'lláh Revealed After the Kitáb-i-Aqdas

THIS is a Tablet sent down by the Lord of mercy that the people of the world may be enabled to draw nigh unto this Ocean which hath surged through the potency of His august Name. Amongst men there are those who have turned away from Him and gainsaid His testimony, while others have quaffed the wine of assurance in the glory of His Name which pervadeth all created things. A grievous loss hath indeed been suffered by those that have inclined their ears to the croaking of the raven, and refused to hearken unto the sweet warblings of the Bird of Heaven singing upon the twigs of the Tree of eternity: Verily there is none other God but Me, the All-Knowing, the All-Wise.

Tablets of Bahá'u'lláh Revealed After the Kitáb-i-Aqdas

Say, by the righteousness of God! The All-Merciful is come invested with power and sovereignty. Through His power the foundations of religions have quaked and the Nightingale of Utterance hath warbled its melody upon the highest branch of true understanding. Verily, He Who was hidden in the knowledge of God and is mentioned in the Holy Scriptures hath appeared.

Tablets of Bahá'u'lláh Revealed After the Kitáb-i-Aqdas

O King! Wert thou to incline thine ears unto the shrill voice of the Pen of Glory and the cooing of the Dove of Eternity, which on the branches of the Lote-Tree beyond which there is no passing, uttereth praises to God, the Maker of all Names and the Creator of earth and heaven, thou wouldst attain unto a station from which thou wouldst behold in the world of being naught save the effulgence of the Adored One, and wouldst regard thy sovereignty as the most contemptible of thy possessions, abandoning it to whosoever might desire it, and setting thy face toward the Horizon aglow with the light of His countenance.

Epistle to the Son of the Wolf

To continue: I have hearkened to the song of the nightingale of knowledge upon the twigs of the tree of thine inmost being, and to the cooing of the dove of certitude upon the branches of the bower of thine heart. Methinks I inhaled the fragrance of purity from the raiment of thy love ... Of this did the nightingale of oneness sing in the garden of his mystical treatise,[1] saying, "And there shall appear upon the tablet of thine heart an inscription of the subtle mysteries of the verse 'Fear ye God; God will teach you', and the bird of thy spirit shall recall the sanctuaries of ancient splendour, and soar upon the wings of longing into the heaven of the command 'Walk the beaten paths of thy Lord', and partake of the choice fruits of communion in the gardens of the utterance 'Feed, moreover, on every kind of fruit.'"[2]

The Call of the Divine Beloved

---

1   Literally, "in the garden of Ghawthíyyih". The *Risáliy-i-Ghawthíyyih* is a mystical treatise by 'Abdu'l-Qádir-i-Gílání (ca. 1077–1166). The sentence that follows is a quotation from this work.

2   Qur'án 2:282, 16:69

He steppeth into the inner sanctuary of the Friend and, as an intimate, shareth the pavilion of the Well-Beloved. He stretcheth forth the hand of truth from the sleeve of the Absolute and revealeth the mysteries of divine power. He seeth in himself neither name nor fame nor rank, but findeth his own praise in the praise of God, and in the name of God beholdeth his own. To him "all songs are from that sovereign King" and every melody from Him. He sitteth on the throne of "Say, all things are of God".[3]

The Call of the Divine Beloved

And if a nightingale soar beyond the clay of self and dwell in the rose bower of the heart, and in Arabian melodies and sweet Persian tones recount the mysteries of God—a single word whereof quickeneth anew every lifeless form and bestoweth the spirit of holiness upon every mouldering bone—thou wilt behold a thousand claws of envy and a myriad talons of hatred hunting after Him and striving with all their power to encompass His death.

The Call of the Divine Beloved

Thus it hath been made clear that these stages depend on the attainment of the wayfarer. In every city he will behold a world, in every valley reach a spring, in every meadow hear a song. But the falcon of the mystic heaven hath many a wondrous carol of the spirit in its breast, and the Persian bird keepeth in its soul many a sweet Arabian melody; yet these are hidden, and hidden shall remain.

The Call of the Divine Beloved

---

3   Qur'án 4:78

The tongue faileth in describing these three valleys, and speech falleth short. The pen steppeth not into this arena, the ink leaveth only a blot. In these stations, the nightingale of the heart hath other songs and secrets, which make the heart to leap and the soul to cry out, but this mystery of inner meaning may be whispered only from heart to heart, and confided only from breast to breast.

The Call of the Divine Beloved

Wert thou to hearken unto the melodies of this mortal Bird, then wouldst thou seek out the eternal and undying chalice and renounce every fleeting and perishable cup. Peace be upon him who followeth the way of guidance!

The Call of the Divine Beloved

O My friend! Listen with heart and soul to the songs of the spirit, and treasure them as thine own eyes; for heavenly wisdoms, even as vernal showers, will not rain forever upon the earth of men's hearts, and though the grace of the All-Bounteous One is never ceasing and never stilled, yet to every time and era a portion is allotted and a bounty assigned, which is vouchsafed in a given measure.

The Call of the Divine Beloved

O Pen of the Most High! Bestir Thyself in remembrance of other kings in this blessed and luminous Book, that perchance they may rise from the couch of heedlessness and give ear unto that which the Nightingale singeth upon the branches of the Divine Lote-Tree, and hasten towards God in this most wondrous and sublime Revelation.

Summons of the Lord of Hosts

O Ancient Beauty! Turn aside from the unbelievers and that which they possess, and waft over all created things the sweet savours of the remembrance of Thy Beloved, the Exalted, the Great. This remembrance quickeneth the world of being and reneweth the temples of all created things. Say: He, verily, hath established Himself upon the Throne of might and glory. Whosoever desireth to gaze upon His countenance, lo, behold Him standing before thee! Blessed be the Lord Who hath revealed Himself in this shining and luminous Beauty. Whosoever desireth to hearken unto His melodies, lo, hear them rising from His resplendent and wondrous lips! And unto whosoever desireth to be illumined by the splendours of His light, say: Seek the court of His presence, for God hath verily granted you leave to approach it, as a token of His grace unto all mankind.

Summons of the Lord of Hosts

I swear by God, O King! Wert thou to incline thine ear to the melodies of that Nightingale which warbleth in manifold accents upon the mystic bough as bidden by thy Lord, the All-Merciful, thou wouldst cast away thy sovereignty and set thy face towards this Scene of transcendent glory, above whose horizon shineth the Book of the Dawntide,[4] and wouldst expend all that thou possessest in thine eagerness to obtain the things of God. Then wouldst thou find thyself raised up to the summit of exaltation and glory, and elevated to the pinnacle of majesty and independence.

Summons of the Lord of Hosts

---

4   Cf. Qur'án 17:78

Say: God is My witness, O concourse of the negligent! We came not unto you to spread disorder in your lands or to sow dissension amongst your peoples. Nay rather, We came in obedience to the command of the sovereign, and in order to exalt your authority, to instruct you in the ways of Our wisdom, and to remind you of that which ye had forgotten—even as He saith in truth: "Warn them, for, in truth, Thy warning will profit the believers."[5] But ye hearkened not unto the sweet melodies of the Spirit, and gave ear unwittingly unto Our enemies, they who follow the promptings of their corrupt inclinations, whose deeds the Evil One hath made fair-seeming in their own eyes, and whose tongues utter calumnies against Us. Heard ye not that which hath been revealed in His all-glorious and unerring Book: "If a wicked man come to you with news, clear it up at once"?[6] Wherefore have ye then cast the command of God behind your backs, and followed in the footsteps of them that are bent on mischief?

Summons of the Lord of Hosts

Say: O people! Is it your wish to conceal the beauty of the Sun behind the veils of your own selfish desires, or to prevent the Spirit from raising its melodies within this sanctified and luminous breast? Fear ye God, and contend not with Him Who representeth the Godhead.

Summons of the Lord of Hosts

Give ear unto that which the Dove of Eternity warbleth upon the twigs of the Divine Lote-Tree: O peoples of the earth!

Summons of the Lord of Hosts

---

5   Qur'án 51:55
6   Qur'án 49:6

Say: O people, do ye imagine that, after rejecting the One through Whom the religions of the world have been made manifest, ye still bear allegiance to the Faith of God? By the righteousness of God! Ye are accounted among the inmates of the Fire. Thus hath the decree been recorded in the Tablets by the Pen of God. Say: Never will the barking of dogs deter the Nightingale from warbling its melodies. Ponder awhile that perchance ye may discover a path leading to the Eternal Truth.
Summons of the Lord of Hosts

Great God! When the stream of utterance reached this stage, We beheld, and lo! the sweet savours of God were being wafted from the dayspring of Revelation, and the morning breeze was blowing out of the Sheba of the Eternal. Its tidings rejoiced anew the heart, and imparted immeasurable gladness to the soul. It made all things new, and brought unnumbered and inestimable gifts from the unknowable Friend. The robe of human praise can never hope to match Its noble stature, and Its shining figure the mantle of utterance can never fit. Without word It unfoldeth the inner mysteries, and without speech It revealeth the secrets of the divine sayings. It teacheth lamentation and moaning to the nightingales warbling upon the bough of remoteness and bereavement, instructeth them in the art of love's ways, and showeth them the secret of heart-surrender.
The Kitáb-i-Íqán

O ye learned of the world! Ye failed to seek Our presence, that ye might hearken unto the sweet melodies of the Spirit and perceive that which God in His bounty hath pleased to bestow upon Me. Verily, this grace hath now escaped you, did ye but know. Had ye sought Our presence, We would have imparted unto you a knowledge that would have rendered you independent of all else.
Summons of the Lord of Hosts

Thus doth the Pen of the Most High warble unto thee its melodies by the leave of thy Lord, the All-Glorious. When thou hast heard and recited them, say: "Praise be unto Thee, O Lord of all the worlds, inasmuch as Thou hast made mention of me through the tongue of Him Who is the Manifestation of Thy Self at a time when He was confined in the Most Great Prison, that the whole world might attain unto true liberty."
Summons of the Lord of Hosts

The answer to all that the distinguished Ṣáḥib hath asked is clear and evident. The intent of that which was sent down in his honour from the heaven of divine providence was that he might give ear to the wondrous melodies of the Dove of Eternity and the gentle murmuring of the inhabitants of the most exalted Paradise, and that he might perceive the sweetness of the call and set foot upon the path.
The Tabernacle of Unity

O servant of God! We have bestowed a dewdrop from the ocean of divine grace; would that men might drink therefrom! We have brought a trace of the sweet melodies of the Beloved; would that men might hearken with their inner ear! Soar upon the wings of joy in the atmosphere of the love of God.
The Tabernacle of Unity

Content with a transitory dominion, they have deprived themselves of an everlasting sovereignty. Thus, their eyes beheld not the light of the countenance of the Well-Beloved, nor did their ears hearken unto the sweet melodies of the Bird of Desire.
The Kitáb-i-Íqán

It is obvious and manifest that the true meaning of the utterances of the Birds of Eternity is revealed to none except those that manifest the Eternal Being, and the melodies of the Nightingale of Holiness can reach no ear save that of the denizens of the everlasting realm.

The Kitáb-i-Íqán

It is evident unto thee that the Birds of Heaven and Doves of Eternity speak a twofold language. One language, the outward language, is devoid of allusions, is unconcealed and unveiled; that it may be a guiding lamp and a beaconing light whereby wayfarers may attain the heights of holiness, and seekers may advance into the realm of eternal reunion. Such are the unveiled traditions and the evident verses already mentioned. The other language is veiled and concealed, so that whatever lieth hidden in the heart of the malevolent may be made manifest and their innermost being be disclosed. Thus hath Sadiq, son of Muhammad, spoken: "God verily will test them and sift them." This is the divine standard, this is the Touchstone of God, wherewith He proveth His servants. None apprehendeth the meaning of these utterances except them whose hearts are assured, whose souls have found favour with God, and whose minds are detached from all else but Him. In such utterances, the literal meaning, as generally understood by the people, is not what hath been intended. Thus it is recorded: "Every knowledge hath seventy meanings, of which one only is known amongst the people. And when the Qá'im shall arise, He shall reveal unto men all that which remaineth." He also saith: "We speak one word, and by it we intend one and seventy meanings; each one of these meanings we can explain."

The Kitáb-i-Íqán

By God! This Bird of Heaven, now dwelling upon the dust, can, besides these melodies, utter a myriad songs, and is able, apart from these utterances, to unfold innumerable mysteries. Every single note of its unpronounced utterances is immeasurably exalted above all that hath already been revealed, and immensely glorified beyond that which hath streamed from this Pen. Let the future disclose the hour when the Brides of inner meaning will, as decreed by the Will of God, hasten forth, unveiled, out of their mystic mansions, and manifest themselves in the ancient realm of being. Nothing whatsoever is possible without His permission; no power can endure save through His power, and there is none other God but He. His is the world of creation, and His the Cause of God. All proclaim His Revelation, and all unfold the mysteries of His Spirit.

The Kitáb-i-Íqán

Inasmuch as it hath been clearly shown that only those who are initiated into the divine mysteries can comprehend the melodies uttered by the Bird of Heaven, it is therefore incumbent upon every one to seek enlightenment from the illumined in heart and from the Treasuries of divine mysteries regarding the intricacies of God's Faith and the abstruse allusions in the utterances of the Day-springs of Holiness. Thus will these mysteries be unravelled, not by the aid of acquired learning, but solely through the assistance of God and the outpourings of His grace. "Ask ye, therefore, of them that have the custody of the Scriptures, if ye know it not."[7]

The Kitáb-i-Íqán

---

7   Qur'án 16:43

At this hour, when the sweet savours of attraction have wafted over Me from the everlasting city, when transports of yearning have seized Me from the land of splendours at the dawning of the Daystar of the worlds above the horizon of 'Iráq, and the sweet melodies of Ḥijáz have brought to Mine ears the mysteries of separation, I have purposed to relate unto thine eminence a portion of that which the Mystic Dove hath warbled in the midmost heart of Paradise as to the true meaning of life and death, though the task be impossible. For were I to interpret these words for thee as it hath been inscribed in the Guarded Tablets, all the books and pages of the world could not contain it, nor could the souls of men bear its weight. I shall nonetheless mention that which beseemeth this day and age, that it might serve as a guidance unto whosoever desireth to gain admittance into the retreats of glory in the realms above, to hearken unto the melodies of the spirit intoned by this divine and mystic bird, and to be numbered with those who have severed themselves from all save God and who in this day rejoice in the presence of their Lord.
Gems of Divine Mysteries

Hearken then unto that which the Bird of Heaven uttered, in the sweetest and most wondrous accents, and in the most perfect and exalted melodies, concerning them—an utterance that shall fill them with remorse from now unto "the day when mankind shall stand before the Lord of the worlds": "Although they had before prayed for victory over those who believed not, yet when there came unto them He of Whom they had knowledge, they disbelieved in Him. The curse of God on the infidels!"[8] Such indeed are their condition and attainments in their vain and empty life. Erelong shall they be cast into the fire of affliction and find none to help or succour them.
Gems of Divine Mysteries

---

8   Qur'án 83:6; 2:89

This is the text of that which was revealed aforetime in the first Gospel, according to Matthew, regarding the signs that must needs herald the advent of the One Who shall come after Him. He saith: "And woe unto them that are with child, and to them that give suck in those days...",[9] until the mystic Dove, singing in the midmost heart of eternity, and the celestial Bird, warbling upon the Divine Lote-Tree, saith: "Immediately after the oppression of those days shall the sun be darkened, and the moon shall not give her light, and the stars shall fall from heaven, and the powers of the heavens shall be shaken: and then shall appear the sign of the Son of man in heaven: and then shall all the tribes of the earth mourn, and they shall see the Son of man coming in the clouds of heaven with power and great glory. And he shall send his angels with a great sound of a trumpet."[10]

Gems of Divine Mysteries

In the second Gospel, according to Mark, the Dove of holiness speaketh in such terms: "For in those days shall be affliction, such as was not from the beginning of the creation which God created unto this time, neither shall be."[11] And it singeth later with the same melodies as before, without change or alteration. God, verily, is a witness unto the truth of My words.

Gems of Divine Mysteries

O My brother! Sanctify thy heart, illumine thy soul, and sharpen thy sight, that thou mayest perceive the sweet accents of the Birds of Heaven and the melodies of the Doves of Holiness warbling in the Kingdom of eternity, and perchance apprehend the inner meaning of these utterances and their

---

9   Matt. 24:19
10 Cf. Matt. 24:29–31
11 Mark 13:19

hidden mysteries. For otherwise, wert thou to interpret these words according to their outward meaning, thou couldst never prove the truth of the Cause of Him Who came after Jesus, nor silence the opponents, nor prevail over the contending disbelievers. For the Christian divines use this verse to prove that the Gospel shall never be abrogated and that, even if all the signs recorded in their Books were fulfilled and the Promised One appeared, He would have no recourse but to rule the people according to the ordinances of the Gospel. They contend that if He were to manifest all the signs indicated in the Books, but decree aught besides that which Jesus had decreed, they would neither acknowledge nor follow Him, so clear and self-evident is this matter in their sight.

Gems of Divine Mysteries

If these wayward souls had indeed paused to reflect upon their conduct, recognized the sweet melodies of that Mystic Dove singing upon the twigs of this snow-white Tree, embraced that which God had revealed unto and bestowed upon them, and discovered the fruits of the Tree of God upon its branches, wherefore then did they reject and denounce Him? Had they not lifted their heads to the heavens to implore His appearance? Had they not besought God at every moment to honour them with His Beauty and sustain them through His presence?

Gems of Divine Mysteries

Incline your ears to the sweet melody of this Prisoner. Arise, and lift up your voices, that haply they that are fast asleep may be awakened. Say: O ye who are as dead! The Hand of Divine bounty proffereth unto you the Water of Life. Hasten and drink your fill. Whoso hath been re-born in this Day, shall never die; whoso remaineth dead, shall never live.

Gleanings from the Writings of Bahá'u'lláh

Strive, O people, to gain admittance into this vast Immensity for which God ordained neither beginning nor end, in which His voice hath been raised, and over which have been wafted the sweet savors of holiness and glory. Divest not yourselves of the Robe of grandeur, neither suffer your hearts to be deprived of remembering your Lord, nor your ears of hearkening unto the sweet melodies of His wondrous, His sublime, His all-compelling, His clear, and most eloquent voice.

Gleanings from the Writings of Bahá'u'lláh

When thou art departed out of the court of My presence, O Muḥammad, direct thy steps towards My House (Baghdád House), and visit it on behalf of thy Lord. When thou reachest its door, stand thou before it and say: Whither is the Ancient Beauty gone, O most great House of God, He through Whom God hath made thee the cynosure of an adoring world, and proclaimed thee to be the sign of His remembrance unto all who are in the heavens and all who are on the earth? Oh! for the former days when thou, O House of God, wert made His footstool, the days when in ceaseless strains the melody of the All-Merciful poured forth from thee! What hath become of thy jewel whose glory hath irradiated all creation? Whither are gone the days in which He, the Ancient King, had made thee the throne of His glory, the days in which He had chosen thee alone to be the lamp of salvation between earth and heaven, and caused thee to diffuse, at dawn and at eventide, the sweet fragrance of the All-Glorious?

Gleanings from the Writings of Bahá'u'lláh

The world is in travail, and its agitation waxeth day by day. Its face is turned towards waywardness and unbelief. Such shall be its plight, that to disclose it now would not be meet and seemly. Its perversity will long continue. And when the appointed hour is come, there shall suddenly appear that which shall cause the limbs of mankind to quake. Then, and only then, will the Divine Standard be unfurled, and the Nightingale of Paradise warble its melody.

Gleanings from the Writings of Bahá'u'lláh

The Pen of Revelation exclaimeth: "On this Day the Kingdom is God's!" The Tongue of Power is calling: "On this Day all sovereignty is, in very deed, with God!" The Phoenix of the realms above crieth out from the immortal Branch: "The glory of all greatness belongeth to God, the Incomparable, the All-Compelling!" The Mystic Dove proclaimeth from its blissful bower, in the everlasting Paradise: "The source of all bounty is derived, in this Day, from God, the One, the Forgiving!" The Bird of the Throne warbleth its melody in its retreats of holiness: "Supreme ascendancy is to be attributed, this Day, to none except God, Him Who hath no peer nor equal, Who is the Most Powerful, the All-Subduing!" The inmost essence of all things voiceth in all things the testimony: "All forgiveness floweth, in this Day, from God, Him to Whom none can compare, with Whom no partners can be joined, the Sovereign Protector of all men, and the Concealer of their sins!" The Quintessence of Glory hath lifted up its voice above My head, and crieth from such heights as neither pen nor tongue can in any degree describe: "God is my witness! He, the Ancient of everlasting days is come, girded with majesty and power. There is none other God but Him, the All-Glorious, the Almighty, the All-Highest, the All-Wise, the All-Pervading, the All-Seeing, the All-Informed, the Sovereign Protector, the Source of eternal light!"

Gleanings from the Writings of Bahá'u'lláh

Say: O people of the Bayán! Did We not admonish you, in all Our Tablets and in all Our hidden Scriptures, not to follow your evil passions and corrupt inclinations, but to keep your eyes directed towards the Scene of transcendent glory, on the Day when the Most Mighty Balance shall be set, the Day when the sweet melodies of the Spirit of God shall be poured out from the right hand of the throne of your Lord, the omnipotent Protector, the All-Powerful, the Holy of Holies? Did We not forbid you to cleave to the things that would shut you out from the Manifestation of our Beauty, in its subsequent Revelation, be they the embodiments of the names of God and all their glory, or the revealers of His attributes and their dominion? Behold, how, as soon as I revealed Myself, ye have rejected My truth and turned away from Me, and been of them that have regarded the signs of God as a play and pastime!

Gleanings from the Writings of Bahá'u'lláh

O Shaykh! Thou hast heard the sweet melodies of the Doves of Utterance cooing on the boughs of the Lote-Tree of knowledge. Hearken, now, unto the notes of the Birds of Wisdom upraised in the Most Sublime Paradise. They verily will acquaint thee with things of which thou wert wholly unaware. Give ear unto that which the Tongue of Might and Power hath spoken in the Books of God, the Desire of every understanding heart. At this moment a Voice was raised from the Lote-Tree beyond which there is no passing, in the heart of the Most Sublime Paradise, bidding Me relate unto thee that which hath been sent down in the Books and Tablets, and the things spoken by My Forerunner, Who laid down His life for this Great Announcement, this Straight Path.

Epistle to the Son of the Wolf

O Shaykh! We have enabled thee to hear the melodies of the Nightingale of Paradise, and unveiled to thine eyes the signs which God, by His all-compelling behest, hath sent down in the Most Great Prison, that thine eye might be cheered, and thy soul be well-assured. He, verily, is the All-Bounteous, the Generous.

Epistle to the Son of the Wolf

Such are the words sung by the Dove of Truth on the boughs of the Divine Lote-Tree. Well is it with him that hath given ear unto its Voice, and quaffed from the oceans of Divine utterance that lie concealed in each of these words. In another connection hath the Voice of the Bayán called aloud from the loftiest branches. He saith—blessed and glorified be He: "In the year nine ye will attain unto all good." On another occasion He saith: "In the year nine ye will attain unto the Presence of God." These melodies, uttered by the Birds of the cities of Knowledge, conform with that which hath been sent down by the All-Merciful in the Qur'án. Blessed are the men of insight; blessed they that attain thereunto.

Epistle to the Son of the Wolf

O Shaykh! Hearken unto the melodies of the Gospel with the ear of fairness. He saith—glorified be His utterance—prophesying the things that are to come: "But of that Day and Hour knoweth no man, no, not the angels of heaven, nor the Son, but the Father." By Father in this connection is meant God—exalted be His glory. He, verily, is the True Educator, and the Spiritual Teacher.

Epistle to the Son of the Wolf

Isaiah saith: "The Lord alone shall be exalted in that Day." Concerning the greatness of the Revelation He saith: "Enter into the rock, and hide thee in the dust, for fear of the Lord, and for the glory of His majesty." And in another connection He saith: "The wilderness and the solitary place shall be glad for them; and the desert shall rejoice, and blossom as the rose. It shall blossom abundantly, and rejoice even with joy and singing: the glory of Lebanon shall be given unto it, the splendor of Carmel and Sharon, they shall see the glory of the Lord, and the splendor of our God."

Epistle to the Son of the Wolf

Ere long, thine eyes will behold the standards of divine power unfurled throughout all regions, and the signs of His triumphant might and sovereignty manifest in every land. As most of the divines have failed to apprehend the meaning of these verses, and have not grasped the significance of the Day of Resurrection, they therefore have foolishly interpreted these verses according to their idle and faulty conception. The one true God is My witness! Little perception is required to enable them to gather from the symbolic language of these two verses all that We have purposed to propound, and thus to attain, through the grace of the All-Merciful, the resplendent morn of certitude. Such are the strains of celestial melody which the immortal Bird of Heaven, warbling upon the Sadrih of Bahá, poureth out upon thee, that, by the permission of God, thou mayest tread the path of divine knowledge and wisdom.

The Kitáb-i-Íqán

This is the day on which the Bird of Utterance hath warbled its melody upon the branches, in the name of its Lord, the God of Mercy. Blessed is the man that hath, on the wings of longing, soared towards God, the Lord of the Judgment Day.

Epistle to the Son of the Wolf

We have created thine eyes to behold the light of My countenance, thine ears to hearken unto the melody of My words, thy body to pay homage before My throne. Do thou render thanks unto God, thy Lord, the Lord of all the world.

Cited in Bahíyyih Khánum the Greatest Holy Leaf, p. 3

I bear witness that thou hast hearkened unto the melody of God and His sweet accents, inclined thine ear to the cooing of the Dove of divine Revelation and hast heard the Nightingale of fidelity pouring forth its notes upon the Branch of Glory: Verily there is none other God but Me, the Incomparable, the All-Informed.

Tablets of Bahá'u'lláh Revealed After the Kitáb-i-Aqdas

The day will surely come when the Nightingale of Paradise will have winged its flight away from its earthly abode unto its heavenly nest. Then will its melody be heard no more, and the beauty of the rose cease to shine. Seize the time, therefore, ere the glory of the divine springtime hath spent itself, and the Bird of Eternity ceased to warble its melody, that thy inner hearing may not be deprived of hearkening unto its call. This is My counsel unto thee and unto the beloved of God. Whosoever wisheth, let him turn thereunto; whosoever wisheth, let him turn away. God, verily, is independent of him and of that which he may see and witness.

These are the melodies, sung by Jesus, Son of Mary, in accents of majestic power in the Riḍván of the Gospel, revealing those signs that must needs herald the advent of the Manifestation after Him ...

The Kitáb-i-Íqán

Furthermore, among the "veils of glory" are such terms as the "Seal of the Prophets" and the like, the removal of which is a supreme achievement in the sight of these base-born and erring souls. All, by reason of these mysterious sayings, these grievous "veils of glory," have been hindered from beholding the light of truth. Have they not heard the melody of that bird of Heaven,[12] uttering this mystery: "A thousand Fátimihs I have espoused, all of whom were the daughters of Muḥammad, Son of 'Abdu'lláh, the 'Seal of the Prophets'"? Behold, how many are the mysteries that lie as yet unravelled within the tabernacle of the knowledge of God, and how numerous the gems of His wisdom that are still concealed in His inviolable treasuries! Shouldest thou ponder this in thine heart, thou wouldst realize that His handiwork knoweth neither beginning nor end. The domain of His decree is too vast for the tongue of mortals to describe, or for the bird of the human mind to traverse; and the dispensations of His providence are too mysterious for the mind of man to comprehend. His creation no end hath overtaken, and it hath ever existed from the "Beginning that hath no beginning"; and the Manifestations of His Beauty no beginning hath beheld, and they will continue to the "End that knoweth no end." Ponder this utterance in thine heart, and reflect how it is applicable unto all these holy Souls.

Likewise, strive thou to comprehend the meaning of the melody of that eternal beauty, Ḥusayn, son of 'Alí, who, addressing Salmán, spoke words such as these: "I was with a thousand Adams, the interval between each and the next Adam was fifty thousand years, and to each one of these I declared the Successorship conferred upon my father." He then recounteth certain details, until he saith: "I have fought one thousand battles in the path of God, the least and most insignificant of which was like the battle of Khaybar, in which

---

12 Imám 'Alí

battle my father fought and contended against the infidels." Endeavour now to apprehend from these two traditions the mysteries of "end," "return," and "creation without beginning or end."

O my beloved! Immeasurably exalted is the celestial Melody above the strivings of human ear to hear or mind to grasp its mystery! How can the helpless ant step into the court of the All-Glorious? And yet, feeble souls, through lack of understanding, reject these abstruse utterances, and question the truth of such traditions. Nay, none can comprehend them save those that are possessed of an understanding heart. Say, He is that End for Whom no end in all the universe can be imagined, and for Whom no beginning in the world of creation can be conceived. Behold, O concourse of the earth, the splendours of the End, revealed in the Manifestations of the Beginning!

The Kitáb-i-Íqán

Let the future disclose what the Judgment of God will ordain, and the Tabernacle of His decree reveal. In such wise We recount unto thee the wonders of the Cause of God, and pour out into thine ears the strains of heavenly melody, that haply thou mayest attain unto the station of true knowledge, and partake of the fruit thereof. Therefore, know thou of a certainty that these Luminaries of heavenly majesty, though their dwelling be in the dust, yet their true habitation is the seat of glory in the realms above. Though bereft of all earthly possessions, yet they soar in the realms of immeasurable riches. And whilst sore tried in the grip of the enemy, they are seated on the right hand of power and celestial dominion. Amidst the darkness of their abasement there shineth upon them the light of unfading glory, and upon their helplessness are showered the tokens of an invincible sovereignty.

The Kitáb-i-Íqán

Thus in moments in which these Essences of being were deeply immersed beneath the oceans of ancient and ever-lasting holiness, or when they soared to the loftiest summits of divine mysteries, they claimed their utterance to be the Voice of divinity, the Call of God Himself. Were the eye of discernment to be opened, it would recognize that in this very state, they have considered themselves utterly effaced and non-existent in the face of Him Who is the All-Pervading, the Incorruptible. Methinks, they have regarded themselves as utter nothingness, and deemed their mention in that Court an act of blasphemy. For the slightest whispering of self, within such a Court, is an evidence of self-assertion and independent existence. In the eyes of them that have attained unto that Court, such a suggestion is itself a grievous transgression. How much more grievous would it be, were aught else to be mentioned in that Presence, were man's heart, his tongue, his mind, or his soul, to be busied with anyone but the Well-Beloved, were his eyes to behold any countenance other than His beauty, were his ear to be inclined to any melody but His voice, and were his feet to tread any way but His way.

The Kitáb-i-Íqán

They that valiantly labour in quest of God's will, when once they have renounced all else but Him, will be so attached and wedded to that City that a moment's separation from it would to them be unthinkable. They will hearken unto infallible proofs from the Hyacinth of that assembly, and receive the surest testimonies from the beauty of its Rose and the melody of its Nightingale. Once in about a thousand years shall this City be renewed and re-adorned.

The Kitáb-i-Íqán

Give ear unto God's holy Voice, and heed thou His sweet and immortal melody.

The Kitáb-i-Íqán

Gracious God! How great is Our amazement at the way the people have gathered around him, and have borne allegiance to his person! Content with transient dust, these people have turned their face unto it, and cast behind their backs Him Who is the Lord of Lords. Satisfied with the croaking of the crow and enamoured with the visage of the raven, they have renounced the melody of the nightingale and the charm of the rose. What unspeakable fallacies the perusal of this pretentious book hath revealed! They are too unworthy for any pen to describe, and too base for one moment's attention. Should a touchstone be found, however, it would instantly distinguish truth from falsehood, light from darkness, and sun from shadow.

The Kitáb-i-Íqán

And, now, strive thou to comprehend the meaning of this saying of 'Alí, the Commander of the Faithful: "Piercing the veils of glory, unaided." Among these "veils of glory" are the divines and doctors living in the days of the Manifestation of God, who, because of their want of discernment and their love and eagerness for leadership, have failed to submit to the Cause of God, nay, have even refused to incline their ears unto the divine Melody. "They have thrust their fingers into their ears."[13] And the people also, utterly ignoring God and taking them for their masters, have placed themselves unreservedly under the authority of these pompous and hypocritical leaders, for they have no sight, no hearing, no heart, of their own to distinguish truth from falsehood.

The Kitáb-i-Íqán

---

13 Qur'án, 2:19

O CHILDREN OF NEGLIGENCE! Set not your affections on mortal sovereignty and rejoice not therein. Ye are even as the unwary bird that with full confidence warbleth upon the bough; till of a sudden the fowler Death throws it upon the dust, and the melody, the form and the color are gone, leaving not a trace. Wherefore take heed, O bondslaves of desire!

The Hidden Words of Bahá'u'lláh, Persian no. 75

O SON OF DUST! Blind thine eyes, that thou mayest behold My beauty; stop thine ears, that thou mayest hearken unto the sweet melody of My voice; empty thyself of all learning, that thou mayest partake of My knowledge; and sanctify thyself from riches, that thou mayest obtain a lasting share from the ocean of My eternal wealth. Blind thine eyes, that is, to all save My beauty; stop thine ears to all save My word; empty thyself of all learning save the knowledge of Me; that with a clear vision, a pure heart and an attentive ear thou mayest enter the court of My holiness.

The Hidden Words of Bahá'u'lláh, Persian no. 11

O MY CHILDREN! I fear lest, bereft of the melody of the dove of heaven, ye will sink back to the shades of utter loss, and, never having gazed upon the beauty of the rose, return to water and clay.

The Hidden Words of Bahá'u'lláh, Persian no. 13

O SON OF SPIRIT! The time cometh, when the nightingale of holiness will no longer unfold the inner mysteries and ye will all be bereft of the celestial melody and of the voice from on high.

The Hidden Words of Bahá'u'lláh, Persian no. 15

The one true God, exalted be His glory, hath wished nothing for Himself. The allegiance of mankind profiteth Him not, neither doth its perversity harm Him. The Bird of the Realm of Utterance voiceth continually this call: "All things have I willed for thee, and thee, too, for thine own sake."

Gleanings from the Writings of Bahá'u'lláh

How unspeakably glorious are the signs, the tokens, the revelations, and splendors which He, Who is the King of Names and Attributes, hath destined for that City! The attainment unto this City quencheth thirst without water, and kindleth the love of God without fire. Within every blade of grass are enshrined the mysteries of an inscrutable Wisdom, and upon every rose-bush a myriad nightingales pour out, in blissful rapture, their melody. Its wondrous tulips unfold the mystery of the undying Fire in the Burning Bush, and its sweet savors of holiness breathe the perfume of the Messianic Spirit. It bestoweth wealth without gold, and conferreth immortality without death. In each one of its leaves ineffable delights are treasured, and within every chamber unnumbered mysteries lie hidden.

Gleanings from the Writings of Bahá'u'lláh

Peace be upon him that inclineth his ear unto the melody of the Mystic Bird calling from the Sadratu'l-Muntahá! Glorified be our Lord, the Most High!

The Kitáb-i-Íqán

O ESSENCE OF NEGLIGENCE! Myriads of mystic tongues find utterance in one speech, and myriads of hidden mysteries are revealed in a single melody; yet, alas, there is no ear to hear, nor heart to understand.

The Hidden Words of Bahá'u'lláh, Persian no. 16

O SON OF BEAUTY! By My spirit and by My favor! By My mercy and by My beauty! All that I have revealed unto thee with the tongue of power, and have written for thee with the pen of might, hath been in accordance with thy capacity and understanding, not with My state and the melody of My voice.
The Hidden Words of Bahá'u'lláh, Arabic no. 67

Hearken ye, O Rulers of America and the Presidents of the Republics therein, unto that which the Dove is warbling on the Branch of Eternity: "There is none other God but Me, the Ever-Abiding, the Forgiving, the All-Bountiful."
The Kitáb-i-Aqdas

From the Prayers of Bahá'u'lláh

He is the King, the All-Knowing, the Wise! Lo, the Nightingale of Paradise singeth upon the twigs of the Tree of Eternity, with holy and sweet melodies, proclaiming to the sincere ones the glad tidings of the nearness of God, calling the believers in the Divine Unity to the court of the Presence of the Generous One, informing the severed ones of the message which hath been revealed by God, the King, the Glorious, the Peerless, guiding the lovers to the seat of sanctity and to this resplendent Beauty ...

Rely upon God, thy God and the Lord of thy fathers. For the people are wandering in the paths of delusion, bereft of discernment to see God with their own eyes, or hear His Melody with their own ears. Thus have We found them, as thou also dost witness.
Tablet of Ahmad

I beseech Thee, by Thine own Self and by Him Whom Thou hast appointed as the Manifestation of Thine own Being and Thy discriminating Word unto all that are in heaven and on earth, to gather together Thy servants beneath the shade of the Tree of Thy gracious providence. Help them, then, to partake of its fruits, to incline their ears to the rustling of its leaves, and to the sweetness of the voice of the Bird that chanteth upon its branches. Thou art, verily, the Help in Peril, the Inaccessible, the Almighty, the Most Bountiful.

Prayers and Meditations by Bahá'u'lláh

Thou art He Who from everlasting was, through the potency of His might, supreme over all things, and, through the operation of His will, was able to ordain all things. Nothing whatsoever, whether in Thy heaven or on Thy earth, can frustrate Thy purpose. Have mercy, then, upon me, O my Lord, through Thy gracious providence and generosity, and incline mine ear to the sweet melodies of the birds that warble their praise of Thee, amidst the branches of the tree of Thy oneness.

Prayers and Meditations by Bahá'u'lláh

Thou seest Me forbidden to speak forth: Then from where will spring Thy melodies, O Nightingale of the worlds?

Fire Tablet

Roll not up, O my Lord, what hath been spread out in Thy name, and extinguish not the lamp which Thine own fire hath lit. Withhold not, O my Lord, the water that is life indeed from running down—the water from whose murmuring the wondrous melodies which extol and glorify Thee can be heard. Deny not, moreover, Thy servants the sweet fragrance of the breath which hath been wafted through Thy love.

Prayers and Meditations by Bahá'u'lláh

Far be it, then, from Thy glory that anyone should gaze on Thy wondrous beauty with any eye save Thine own eye, or hear the melodies proclaiming Thine almighty sovereignty with any ear except Thine own ear. Too high art Thou exalted for the eye of any creature to behold Thy beauty, or for the understanding of any heart to scale the heights of Thine immeasurable knowledge.

Prayers and Meditations by Bahá'u'lláh

Enrapture him, moreover, with the sweet melodies of Him Who is the Fountain-Head of Thy Revelation, in such wise that he may wholly surrender his will to Thy pleasure, and fix his hopes upon the things Thou didst ordain in Thy Tablets.

Prayers and Meditations by Bahá'u'lláh

Cause them to be so enraptured by the sweetness of Thy divine melodies that they will rid themselves of all attachment to any one except Thee, and will turn wholly towards Thee, and extol Thee under all conditions, saying: "Praised be Thou, O Lord our God, inasmuch as Thou hast enabled us to recognize Thy most exalted and all-glorious Self..."

Prayers and Meditations by Bahá'u'lláh

I beseech Thee, by Thy Most Great Name, to open the eyes of Thy servants, that they may behold Thee shining above the horizon of Thy majesty and glory, and that they may not be hindered by the croaking of the raven from hearkening to the voice of the Dove of Thy sublime oneness, nor be prevented by the corrupt waters from partaking of the pure wine of Thy bounty and the everlasting streams of Thy gifts.

Prayers and Meditations by Bahá'u'lláh

Thou beholdest, O my God, how every bone in my body soundeth like a pipe with the music of Thine inspiration, revealing the signs of Thy oneness and the clear tokens of Thy unity. I entreat Thee, O my God, by Thy Name which irradiateth all things, to raise up such servants as shall incline their ears to the voice of the melodies that hath ascended from the right hand of the throne of Thy glory. Make them, then, to quaff from the hand of Thy grace the wine of Thy mercy, that it may assure their hearts, and cause them to turn away from the left hand of idle fancies and vain imaginings to the right hand of confidence and certitude.

Prayers and Meditations by Bahá'u'lláh

Having testified, therefore, unto mine own impotence and the impotence of Thy servants, I beseech Thee, by the brightness of the light of Thy beauty, not to refuse Thy creatures attainment to the shores of Thy most holy ocean. Draw them, then, O my God, through the Divine sweetness of Thy melodies, towards the throne of Thy glory and the seat of Thine eternal holiness. Thou art, verily, the Most Powerful, the Supreme Ruler, the Great Giver, the Most Exalted, the Ever-Desired.

Prayers and Meditations by Bahá'u'lláh

I implore Thee by Thine All-Glorious Name, wherewith Thou didst adorn all the denizens of the kingdom of Thy revelation and the inmates of the heaven of Thy will, to grant that my soul may be attracted by the sweetness of the melody of the Bird of Heaven that chanteth amidst the branches of the tree of Thy decree that Thou art God, that there is none other God beside Thee.

Prayers and Meditations by Bahá'u'lláh

Magnified be Thy name, O Lord my God! Behold Thou mine eye expectant to gaze on the wonders of Thy mercy, and mine ear longing to hearken unto Thy sweet melodies, and my heart yearning for the living waters of Thy knowledge. Thou seest Thy handmaiden, O my God, standing before the habitation of Thy mercy, and calling upon Thee by Thy name which Thou hast chosen above all other names and set up over all that are in heaven and on earth. Send down upon her the breaths of Thy mercy, that she may be carried away wholly from herself, and be drawn entirely towards the seat which, resplendent with the glory of Thy face, sheddeth afar the radiance of Thy sovereignty, and is established as Thy throne. Potent art Thou to do what Thou willest. No God is there beside Thee, the All-Glorious, the Most Bountiful.

Prayers and Meditations by Bahá'u'lláh

Purge out thoroughly their ears, O my Lord, that they may hearken unto the sweet melodies that have ascended from the right hand of the throne of Thy glory. I swear by Thy might! Were any one to attune his ears to their harmony he would soar up to the kingdom of Thy revelation, wherein every created thing proclaimeth that Thou art God, and that there is none other God save Thee, the Omnipotent, the Help in Peril, the Self-Subsisting. Cleanse Thou, O my God, the eyes of Thy servants, and so transport them by the sweetness of Thine utterances that calamities will be powerless to hinder them from turning unto Thee, and from directing their eyes towards the horizon of Thy Revelation.

Prayers and Meditations by Bahá'u'lláh

Lulled by the cooing of the Dove of Thine Eternity, suffer me to sleep, for woes at their blackest have befallen me.

Prayers and Meditations by Bahá'u'lláh

Create in me a pure heart, O my God, and renew a tranquil conscience within me, O my Hope! Through the spirit of power confirm Thou me in Thy Cause, O my Best-Beloved, and by the light of Thy glory reveal unto me Thy path, O Thou the Goal of my desire! Through the power of Thy transcendent might lift me up unto the heaven of Thy holiness, O Source of my being, and by the breezes of Thine eternity gladden me, O Thou Who art my God! Let Thine everlasting melodies breathe tranquillity on me, O my Companion, and let the riches of Thine ancient countenance deliver me from all except Thee, O my Master, and let the tidings of the revelation of Thine incorruptible Essence bring me joy, O Thou Who art the most manifest of the manifest and the most hidden of the hidden!

Prayers and Meditations by Bahá'u'lláh

Lauded and glorified art Thou, O my God! I entreat Thee by the sighing of Thy lovers and by the tears shed by them that long to behold Thee, not to withhold from me Thy tender mercies in Thy Day, nor to deprive me of the melodies of the Dove that extolleth Thy oneness before the light that shineth from Thy face.

Prayers and Meditations by Bahá'u'lláh

Graciously assist me, O my God, in the days of the Manifestation of Thy Cause and of the Day-Spring of Thy Revelation, to tear asunder the veils which have hindered me from recognizing Thee, and from immersing myself beneath the ocean of Thy knowledge. Hold Thou me with the hands of Thy power, and grant that I may be so carried away by the sweet melodies of the Dove of Thy oneness, that I will cease to regard in all creation any face except Thy face, O Thou the Goal of my desire, and will recognize in the visible world naught else save the evidences of Thy might, O Thou Who art the God of mercy!

Prayers and Meditations by Bahá'u'lláh

From the fragrant breezes of Thy joy let a breath pass over me, O my Goal, and into the heights of the paradise of Thy reality let me gain admission, O my Adored One! To the melodies of the dove of Thy oneness suffer me to hearken, O Resplendent One, and through the spirit of Thy power and Thy might quicken me, O my Provider!

Prayers and Meditations by Bahá'u'lláh

Sanctify, then, their eyes, O my God, that they may behold the light of Thy Beauty, and purge their ears, that they may listen to the melodies of the Dove of Thy transcendent oneness. Flood, then, their hearts with the wonders of Thy love, and preserve their tongues from mentioning any one save Thee, and guard their faces from turning to aught else except Thyself. Potent art Thou to do what pleaseth Thee. Thou, verily, art the Almighty, the Help in Peril, the Self-Subsisting.

Prayers and Meditations by Bahá'u'lláh

I yield Thee such thanks as can enable the Heavenly Dove to warble forth, upon the branches of the Lote-Tree of Immortality, her song: "Verily, Thou art God. No God is there besides Thee. From eternity Thou hast been exalted above the praise of aught else but Thee, and been high above the description of any one except Thyself." I yield Thee such thanks as can cause the Nightingale of Glory to pour forth its melody in the highest heaven: "'Alí (the Báb), in truth, is Thy servant, Whom Thou hast singled out from among Thy Messengers and Thy chosen Ones, and made Him to be the Manifestation of Thyself in all that pertaineth unto Thee, and that concerneth the revelation of Thine attributes and the evidences of Thy names."

Prayers and Meditations by Bahá'u'lláh

How great is Thy power! How exalted Thy sovereignty! How lofty Thy might! How excellent Thy majesty! How supreme is Thy grandeur—a grandeur which He Who is Thy Manifestation hath made known and wherewith Thou hast invested Him as a sign of Thy generosity and bountiful favor. I bear witness, O my God, that through Him Thy most resplendent signs have been uncovered, and Thy mercy hath encompassed the entire creation. But for Him, how could the Celestial Dove have uttered its songs or the Heavenly Nightingale, according to the decree of God, have warbled its melody?

Prayers and Meditations by Bahá'u'lláh

Glorified art Thou, O Lord my God! I call upon Thee at this time when the accents of the dove of separation are raised from the land of Iraq, and the warbling of the Nightingale of fervent longing is heard from the horizon of the world—at such a time do I call upon Thee, proclaiming: "Thou in truth art God, the King, the Mighty, the Beauteous. From everlasting, O my God, Thou hast been exalted in the supremacy of Thy might, Thy power, and Thy glory, and unto all eternity Thou wilt remain transcendent in the sublimity of Thy grandeur, Thy majesty, and Thy splendour. Every Prophet is filled with consternation when confronted by the manifold evidences of Thy wrath, and every Chosen One standeth dismayed before the revelations of Thy might. No God is there but Thee, the Almighty, the All-Powerful, the All-Compelling."

Additional Prayers Revealed by Bahá'u'lláh

From the Writings of the Báb

Recite ye as much as convenient from this Qur'án both at morn and at eventide, and chant the verses of this Book, by the leave of the eternal God, in the sweet accents of this Bird which warbleth its melody in the vault of heaven.

Selections from the Writings of the Báb

Immeasurably glorified and exalted art Thou! That which alone beseemeth Thee is the befitting mention made by Thine Own Self, and that only which is worthy of Thee is the anthem of praise voiced by Thine Own Essence ...

Selections from the Writings of the Báb

From the Writings of 'Abdu'l-Bahá

Let us seek the song with the sweetest strains, so that it may be taken up by the angels and carried to the supreme concourse. Let us hearken to the melody which will stir the world of humanity, so that the people may be transformed with joy. Let us listen to a symphony which will confer life on man; then we can obtain universal results; then we shall receive a new spirit; then we shall become illumined. Let us investigate a song which is above all songs; one which will develop the spirit and produce harmony and exhilaration, unfolding the inner potentialities of life.

Divine Philosophy

These servants were noble souls, and these radiant hearts were made illumined and resplendent through the light of Thy guidance. They drank a brimming cup of the wine of Thy love, and gave ear to eternal mysteries imparted by the melodies of Thy knowledge.

Twenty-six Prayers Revealed by 'Abdu'l-Bahá

O ye beloved of the Merciful! The Abhá Beauty hath shone forth with His manifold names and attributes from the Dawning-Point of all desires. He hath caused this glorious century to become the revealer of His wondrous grace through the effulgence of this new light, and hath set aglow the candle of unity in the world of being. In sweet accents of oneness and in celestial melodies proclaiming Divine Unity, He hath warbled upon the branches of the garden of inner meanings so as to gather the scattered peoples of the world under the shadow of the Word of God and bring the hostile and contentious tribes of the earth together in unity and harmony beneath the canopy of the love of God.

Light of the World

The four pages in the blessed handwriting of the Báb—may my life be a sacrifice unto Him—that thou didst present to 'Abdu'l-Bahá as a gift were received. Thereupon, the very walls resounded with the anthem of "O blessed, blessed are we!" whilst 'Abdu'l-Bahá hearkened from a corner unto these sweet melodies. Well done! Well done! for having cheered our hearts with such a cherished gift.

Light of the World

O thou who art firm in the Covenant! The opening of thy letter bore the words "O 'Abdu'l- Bahá!" What a call this was, for it caused my heart to leap with joy and my soul to tremble with delight. Glad-tidings encircled me on every side, my eyes were cheered, and my whole being breathed in the sweet savours of a garden of roses. This call, even as the melody of the Concourse on high, filled the soul of 'Abdu'l-Bahá with joy and rapture.

By Him Who hath illumined my face with the light of absolute servitude to His Holy Threshold! No melody can fill this yearning soul with such joy and rapture as the call of "O 'Abdu'l-Bahá!" And no sweet accents warbled by the birds of the orchards can thrill my heart with such delight as the dulcet tune of "O 'Abdu'l-Bahá!" This melody causeth my heart to leap with joy, and these wondrous words fill me with blissful rapture, but only on condition that this name be accompanied by no other epithets of praise, and paired with no other titles. The designation should be "'Abdu'l-Bahá" alone for it to bestow boundless joy upon my heart and soul. This is my qualification and my station, this is my title and my glory, and this indeed is my highest aspiration throughout eternity.

Light of the World

But know this: The lamp of God shall be lit, and His brilliant star shall shine upon the assemblage of humanity. His ocean shall surge, and the leviathan of the heavenly sea shall roar. The songbird of the rose-garden of Bahá shall warble with blissful rapture, and the nightingale of the bower of the Lord shall chant its eternal song. Thereupon shall the hearing ear, attuned to the song of the nightingale, hearken to the divine call, proclaiming: "Sanctified be the Lord! This is the songster of My paradise! This is the nightingale of My rose-garden! This is the candle of My worlds!" The glory of God rest upon thee.

Light of the World

O friends! Praise be to God that the banner of Divine Unity hath been hoisted in every land, and the melody of the Abhá Kingdom hath been raised on every side. The holy Seraph of the Concourse on high is raising the cry of "Yá Bahá'u'l-Abhá!" in the midmost heart of the world, and the power of the Word of God is breathing true life into the body of existence.
Light of the World

O thou who art kindled by the fire of the Love of God!
Rejoice through the fragrance of God and be attracted by the melodies of the holy birds in the garden of the gifts of God!
Tablets of 'Abdu'l-Bahá 'Abbás, vol. 1

And now shall come to pass even greater things than these, for this is the summons of the Lord of Hosts, this is the trumpet-call of the living Lord, this is the anthem of world peace, this is the standard of righteousness and trust and understanding raised up among all the variegated peoples of the globe; this is the splendour of the Sun of Truth, this is the holiness of the spirit of God Himself.
Selections from the Writings of 'Abdu'l-Bahá

O ye who are the chosen ones of the Abhá Kingdom! Praise ye the Lord of Hosts for He, riding upon the clouds, hath come down to this world out of the heaven of the invisible realm, so that East and West were lit by the glory of the Sun of Truth, and the call of the Kingdom was raised, and the heralds of the realm above, with melodies of the Concourse on high, sang out the glad tidings of the Coming.
Selections from the Writings of 'Abdu'l-Bahá

DAY and night I have no other occupation than the remembrance of the friends, praying from the depth of my heart in their behalf, begging for them confirmation from the Kingdom of God and supplicating the direct effect of the breaths of the Holy Spirit. I am hopeful from the favors of His Highness the Lord of Bestowals, that the friends of God during such a time may become the secret cause of the illumination of the hearts of humanity, breathing the breath of life upon the spirits—whose praiseworthy results may become conducive to the glory and exaltation of humankind throughout all eternity. Although in some of the Western States, like California, Oregon, Washington and Colorado, the fragrances of holiness are diffused, numerous souls have taken a share and a portion from the fountain of everlasting life, they have obtained heavenly benediction, have drunk an overflowing cup from the wine of the love of God and have hearkened to the melody of the Supreme Concourse—yet in the states of New Mexico, Wyoming, Montana, Idaho, Utah, Arizona and Nevada, the lamp of the love of God is not ignited in a befitting and behooving manner, and the call of the Kingdom of God has not been raised. Now, if it is possible, show ye an effort in this direction. Either travel yourselves, personally, throughout those states or choose others and send them, so that they may teach the souls. For the present those states are like unto dead bodies: they must breathe into them the breath of life and bestow upon them a heavenly spirit. Like unto the stars they must shine in that horizon and thus the rays of the Sun of Reality may also illumine those states.

Tablets of the Divine Plan

O ye beloved of 'Abdu'l-Bahá and ye handmaids of the Merciful! It is early morning, and the reviving winds of the Abhá Paradise are blowing over all creation, but they can stir only the pure of heart, and only the pure sense can detect their fragrance. Only the perceiving eye beholdeth the rays of the sun; only the listening ear can hear the singing of the Concourse on high.

Selections from the Writings of 'Abdu'l-Bahá

Now California and the other Western States must earn an ideal similarity with the Holy Land, and from that state and that region the breaths of the Holy Spirit be diffused to all parts of America and Europe, that the call of the Kingdom of God may exhilarate and rejoice all the ears, the divine principles bestow a new life, the different parties may become one party, the divergent ideas may disappear and revolve around one unique center, the East and the West of America may embrace each other, the anthem of the oneness of the world of humanity may confer a new life upon all the children of men, and the tabernacle of universal peace be pitched on the apex of America; thus Europe and Africa may become vivified with the breaths of the Holy Spirit, this world may become another world ...

Tablets of the Divine Plan

Are you pleased to receive such a guest, freed from his prison to bring the glorious Message to you? He who never could have thought such a meeting possible! Now by the Grace of God, by His wonderful Power, I, who was condemned to perpetual imprisonment in a far off town of the East, am here in Paris talking with you!

Henceforward we shall always be together, heart and soul and spirit, pressing forward in the work till all men are gathered together under the tent of the Kingdom, singing the songs of peace.

Paris Talks

Fifth: The first Mashriqu'l-Adhkár in America was instituted in Chicago, and this honor and distinction is infinite in value. Out of this Mashriqu'l-Adhkár, without doubt, thousands of Mashriqu'l-Adhkárs will be born.

Likewise (were instituted in Chicago) the general Annual Conventions, the foundation of the Star of the West, the Publishing Society for the publication of books and Tablets and their circulation in all parts of America, and the preparations now under way for the celebration of the Golden Centenary Anniversary of the Kingdom of God. I hope that this Jubilee and this Exhibition may be celebrated in the utmost perfection so that the call to the world of unity, "There is no God but One God, and all the Messengers, from the beginning to the Seal of the Prophets (Muḥammad) were sent on the part of the True One!" may be raised; the flag of the oneness of the world of humanity be unfurled, the melody of universal peace may reach the ears of the East and the West, all the paths may be cleared and straightened, all the hearts may be attracted to the Kingdom of God, the tabernacle of unity be pitched on the apex of America, the song of the love of God may exhilarate and rejoice all the nations and peoples, the surface of the earth may become the eternal paradise, the dark clouds may be dispelled and the Sun of Truth may shine forth with the utmost intensity ...

Continually my ear and eye are turned toward the Central States; perchance a melody from some blessed souls may reach my ears—souls who are the dawning-places of the love of God, the stars of the horizon of sanctification and holiness—souls who will illumine this dark universe and quicken to life this dead world. The joy of 'Abdu'l-Bahá depends upon this! I hope that you may become confirmed therein.

Consequently, those souls who are in a condition of the utmost severance, purified from the defects of the world of nature, sanctified from attachment to this earth, vivified

with the breaths of eternal life—with luminous hearts, with heavenly spirit, with attraction of consciousness, with celestial magnanimity, with eloquent tongues and with clear explanations—such souls must hasten and travel through all parts of the Central States. In every city and village they must occupy themselves with the diffusion of the divine exhortations and advices, guide the souls and promote the oneness of the world of humanity. They must play the melody of international conciliation with such power that every deaf one may attain hearing, every extinct person may be set aglow, every dead one may obtain new life and every indifferent soul may find ecstasy. It is certain that such will be the consummation.
Tablets of the Divine Plan

O ye friends!

Thank God that the Light of Truth shone in that city, the bounty of guidance was granted, the fire of the love of God was ignited and the veil of superstition was burned away.

Some souls have arisen who have unsealed their eyes, unstopped their ears, witnessed the great signs and heard the eternal melody of the Supreme Concourse. Each of them became a faithful tree in the orchard of the love of God and a shining luminous star in the horizon of the knowledge of God. This is from the eternal bounty and the everlasting gift.

I entreat and supplicate in the Threshold of the Almighty and ask for your confirmation and assistance, that you may be born wholly out of the physical world into the Realm Divine, to seek after the eternal life and wish for the everlasting gift, so that you may shine upon ages and cycles like unto the morning star!
Tablets of ʻAbduʼl-Bahá ʻAbbás, vol. 3

Praise be to God that the divine outpourings are infinite, the melody of the lordly principles is in the utmost efficacy, the most great Orb shining with perfect splendor, the cohorts of the Supreme Concourse are attacking with invincible power, the tongues are sharper than the swords, the hearts are more brilliant than the light of electricity, the magnanimity of the friends precedes all the magnanimities of the former and subsequent generations, the souls are divinely attracted, and the fire of the love of God is enkindled.

At this time and at this period we must avail ourselves of this most great opportunity. We must not sit inactive for one moment; we must sever ourselves from composure, rest, tranquillity, goods, property, life and attachment to material things. We must sacrifice everything to His Highness, the Possessor of existence, so that the powers of the Kingdom may show greater penetration and the brilliant effulgence in this New Cycle may illumine the worlds of minds and ideals.

It is about twenty-three years that the fragrances of God have been diffused in America, but no adequate and befitting motion has been realized, and no great acclamation and acceleration has been witnessed. Now it is my hope that through the heavenly power, the fragrances of the Merciful, the attraction of consciousness, the celestial outpourings, the heavenly cohorts and the gushing forth of the fountain of divine love, the believers of God may arise and in a short time the greatest good may unveil her countenance, the Sun of Reality may shine forth with such intensity that the darkness of the world of nature may become entirely dispelled and driven away; from every corner a most wonderful melody may be raised, the morning birds may break into such a song that the world of humanity may be quickened and moved, the solid bodies may become liquefied, and the souls who are like unto adamantine rocks may open their wings and through the heat of the love of God fly heavenward.

Tablets of the Divine Plan

But these stories did not have any effect on the resolution of 'Abdu'l-Bahá. He, trusting in God, turned his face toward Montreal. When he entered that city he observed all the doors open, he found the hearts in the utmost receptivity and the ideal power of the Kingdom of God removing every obstacle and obstruction. In the churches and meetings of that Dominion he called men to the Kingdom of God with the utmost joy, and scattered such seeds which will be irrigated with the hand of divine power. Undoubtedly those seeds will grow, becoming green and verdant, and many rich harvests will be gathered. In the promotion of the divine principles he found no antagonist and no adversary. The believers he met in that city were in the utmost spirituality, and attracted with the fragrances of God. He found that through the effort of the maidservant of God Mrs. Maxwell a number of the sons and daughters of the Kingdom in that Dominion were gathered together and associated with each other, increasing this joyous exhilaration day by day. The time of sojourn was limited to a number of days, but the results in the future are inexhaustible. When a farmer comes into the possession of a virgin soil, in a short time he will bring under cultivation a large field. Therefore I hope that in the future Montreal may become so stirred, that the melody of the Kingdom may travel to all parts of the world from that Dominion and the breaths of the Holy Spirit may spread from that center to the East and the West of America.

Tablets of the Divine Plan

O Lord of Hosts! Confirm Thine affectionate … in Thy servitude, aid him in the service of Thy Word, open to his face the door of knowledge, reveal to his heart the realities and significances, and grant him the ecstasy of the cup of reality, gladden him through the melody of Thy love, make his night, day, and day, happy!

Tablets of 'Abdu'l-Bahá 'Abbás, vol. 2

Consider ye! In the day of His Highness Christ, the grandeur and majesty of their Holiness the Apostles, was not known. After three-hundred years the loftiness of the station and the exaltation of their attainment became manifest. Ere long the result of the deeds in this cycle of Baha'o'llah will appear and every one of the friends and the maid-servants will be crowned with a diadem whose splendid gems will radiate brilliancy and effulgence throughout cycles and ages.

Therefore, O ye servants of God and the maid-servants of the Merciful One, do ye not rest for one moment! Do ye not seek any composure! Do ye not wish for any rest and ease! Endeavor and make ye an effort with all your heart and soul to spread the fragrances of Paradise, to raise the eternal melody of the Kingdom of Abha, to establish the gathering of fellowship, to become assisted with the confirmations of the Holy Spirit; to clothe the temple of existence with a new garment; to bestow eternal life upon the reality of souls; to become a cause of the civilization of the human world; to characterize the bloodthirsty animals with the heavenly attributes and divine commemorations; to pacify the world with peace and salvation, and to adorn man with the favors of His Highness the Merciful One; that perchance ignorance, animosity and strangeness may be removed entirely from among the denizens of the world, and the Banner of Reconciliation, Freedom, Nobleness and Oneness be hoisted; for the chains of existence contain countless links, each connected with the other. This connection is the cause of the appearance of the invisible powers in the world of the visible.

Tablets of 'Abdu'l-Bahá 'Abbás, vol. 3

O thou servant of the True One!

Thy letter was received. The meeting ... which was arranged with the utmost union in the studio of Miss ... was in reality spiritual, merciful and illumined. The friends of God were associating with great harmony and friendship. I hope that all the people of the world become united and cemented. The Blessed Perfection hath appeared for the sole purpose of the unification and solidarity of the people of the world, so that all of them may enter under the shade of one tree, sing one melody in one rose-garden and adorn the universe with love and oneness.

Every meeting which is organized for the purpose of unity and concord will be conducive to changing strangers into friends, enemies into associated, and Abdul-Baha will be present in his heart and soul with that meeting.

I entreat from God that the believers may at all times strive to bring about union and harmony, in order that this power of unity may display an effect in this world; each country become illuminated, the darkness of foreignness be dispelled gradually and the light of unanimity dawn and shed its rays to all parts.

Tablets of 'Abdu'l-Bahá 'Abbás, vol. 3

The tree will grow, the earth will send forth hyacinths[14] and give blessings, and man will become of the heavenly angels. Feed on the light of guidance and impart light to the people. The bird will warble melodies unknown save by the birds of heaven; then tear asunder the veil and see the realities of things with the eye of God. Verily, thy Lord guideth whomsoever He willeth unto the Straight Path!

The Promised Spot will be made a racecourse for the steeds of the race of Knowledge and the lights of the Merciful will shine upon it. The dispersed ones will return to the Center of Gathering and the birds will return from the meadows of the world unto the Nest of Harmony. This is a preordained matter.

Tablets of 'Abdu'l-Bahá 'Abbás, vol. 3

---

14 Symbol of knowledge

Briefly, four days and four nights were they the guests in the house of this imprisoned one, continually praising and commending the beloved of God and giving the glad-tidings of the attraction of the friends with the fragrances of God. In this prison, Abdul-Baha hath no happiness except the arrival of the good news of the believers. Whenever one praises them, the heart is dilated and the soul is rejoiced.

Therefore, O ye companions of Abdul-Baha, display ye an effort, so that ye may make that region (America) the Paradise of Abha, hoisting the banner of the Most Great Peace and spreading the teachings of the Beauty of Abha; in order that the slumbrous world become awakened, the unconscious become mindful, the universe become another universe, the human world become the realm of the Kingdom, earthly emotions become heavenly attractions, cruelty and oppression be changed into love and faithfulness, the clattering of the sword be transformed into the sweet melody of the pen and the discordant sound of war become the wonderful song of love and intelligence; in order that all the individuals of humanity embrace each other and live among themselves in perfect love and affinity.

Tablets of 'Abdu'l-Bahá 'Abbás, vol. 3

Know thou that some of the souls who arrive at this Blessed Spot possess hearing, seeing and smelling; they see what no eye hath ever seen, they hear the melodies of the Dove of Holiness on the Tree of Life, they inhale the fragrances of God from this Garden, and they surely realize that, verily, this Blessed Spot is a center for pure seeing and strong hearing and is the direction from which the breezes of the Holy Spirit blow.

Tablets of 'Abdu'l-Bahá 'Abbás, vol. 3

Remove not, O Lord, the festal board that hath been spread in Thy Name, and extinguish not the burning flame that hath been kindled by Thine unquenchable fire. Withhold not from flowing that living water of Thine that murmureth with the melody of Thy glory and Thy remembrance, and deprive not Thy servants from the fragrance of Thy sweet savors breathing forth the perfume of Thy love.

Bahá'í Prayers

The anthem of the Abhá Kingdom can be heard from the celestial Concourse:

… The sweetly singing mystic bird, upon a verdant cypress bough, imparteth knowledge to the soul;

Commit His secrets to thy heart! Commit His secrets to thy heart!

Light of the World

O thou spiritual clarion!

The voice of the physical clarion may travel the distance of three miles, but the harmony of the spiritual Clarion reacheth to the East and the West. The effect of that is only in the bodies; but the effect of this is in the spirits. The first proclaimeth the time of prayer; the second announceth the appearance of the Most Great Resurrection. That hath no conscious knowledge of its own voice; while this is exhilarated and rejoiced by its own melody.

How significant and eloquent were those new verses, for they were the notes of the clarion of the love of God.

Raise thou this call as much as thou canst, and sound and blow this clarion continually night and day, so that the souls may become quickened and the people find eternal life.

Tablets of 'Abdu'l-Bahá 'Abbás, vol. 1

The doors of the Kingdom are opened; O what good news to those who advance! The garden of paradise is drawn near; O what a pleasure to those who enter! The dove of holiness is cooing; O what a happiness to those who hear! The gates of heaven are open; blessed are they who see! The hosts of angels are standing in battle order; what a joy to those who gain the victory! The trumpet of life is sounding; how good it is to those who are awake!

Tablets of 'Abdu'l-Bahá 'Abbás, vol. 3

Thou hast written that thou lovest the Bible. Undoubtedly, the friends and the maid-servants of the Merciful should know the value of the Bible, for they are the ones who have discovered its real significances and have become cognizant of the hidden mystery of the Holy Book.

Deliver my greeting to ... and say: "I supplicate God that thou mayest gladden and rejoice the heart of ... with the melody of the Kingdom, rend asunder the veil of her concealment, enlighten her face with the light of the Most Great Guidance and make her eyes see and her ears hear."

Tablets of 'Abdu'l-Bahá 'Abbás, vol. 1

O ye dear friends of Abdul-Baha! It is some time since any heart-thrilling melody hath reached the ear of life from certain countries, and life and conscience have not found happiness and joy. Howbeit all are remembered at all times and are indeed present before the sight. For, verily, the chalice of the heart is overflowing with the wine of the love of the friends; and their attachment and the desire to see them flow and circulate in the veins and arteries, even as the spirit.

Tablets of 'Abdu'l-Bahá 'Abbás, vol. 2

O ye beloved servants of Abdul-Baha and the maid-servants of the Merciful One! It is the early dawn and the soul-refreshing breeze of the Paradise of Abha is wafting upon all the contingent beings, but it displays the effect only in pure hearts and perfumes only the healthy mind. A seeing eye beholdeth the splendors of the sun and a hearing ear listeneth to the melody of the Supreme Concourse.

Tablets of ʿAbdu'l-Bahá ʿAbbás, vol. 2

In brief, arise thou in the service of thy Lord with the utmost firmness and steadfastness. I was very much pleased with thee. Undoubtedly this favor will become the cause of the greatest development for thee.

Likewise, thou and his honor Mirza ... are two brothers and like unto two birds living in one nest and singing one melody.

Tablets of ʿAbdu'l-Bahá ʿAbbás, vol. 2

Announce on my behalf longing greeting to Mr ... and say, "The melody of the Kingdom is that which hath caused the motion of the universe; the musk-diffusing fragrance of the rose-garden of God is that which hath perfumed the nostrils; and the reflection of the Sun of Truth is that which hath illumined the whole earth. Now is the beginning of illumination! ..."

Tablets of ʿAbdu'l-Bahá ʿAbbás, vol. 1

On that night thy house was the nest and the shelter of the birds of God. The divine melodies and the celestial lyres made that place a feast of heaven and an assembly of the Kingdom. Abdul-Baha was present there in heart and soul and was joyful and happy. Thank thou God.

Tablets of ʿAbdu'l-Bahá ʿAbbás, vol. 1

O ye beloved of God! As long as ye can strive to set aglow the hearts with love, be attracted to one another and be members of each other. Every soul of the beloved ones must adore the other and withhold not his possession and life from them, and by all means he must endeavor to make that other joyous and happy. But that other (the recipient of such love) must also be disinterested and life-sacrificing. Thus may this Sunrise flood the horizons, this melody gladden and make happy all the people, this divine remedy become the panacea for every disease, this Spirit of Reality become the cause of life for every soul.

O ye friends and maid-servants of the Merciful! It is life-offering, rejoicing, happiness and the manifestation of Divine Favors.

Tablets of 'Abdu'l-Bahá 'Abbás, vol. 1

As to the wonderful melody whereby thy spirit was revived, verily it is a melody of the melodies of the divine music, which will cause the spirits to ascend unto the Supreme Horizon and will (cause) the mysteries to be unfolded.

O maid-servant of God! Be one of the angels of peace and a saint in the world. Verily thy Lord will cause thee to listen to that wonderful melody, through the spiritual instrument.

Tablets of 'Abdu'l-Bahá 'Abbás, vol. 1

O Thou kind God! That scattered assembly[15] is Thine, and that gathering of friends is of Thee. Their eyes are opened, their hearts in tune with Thy love, and their ears in communion with Thy hidden mysteries.

O Thou who art self-sufficient! Let a beautiful song reach this people from the birds of that garden, that they may warble, rejoice and be happy, implore and supplicate the Lord.

Tablets of 'Abdu'l-Bahá 'Abbás, vol. 1

---

15 American believers

Verily, I beg of God to ordain for thee in the future to come to this Blessed and White Land, to cause thee to hear the melodies of the Dove and to grant that thou mayest present thyself before the hands of Abdul-Baha.

Tablets of 'Abdu'l-Bahá 'Abbás, vol. 1

O maid-servant of God! The radiance of favor is (cast) upon thy head and thou art clad with the robe of gift. Praise be unto God, that the breeze of the divine spring maketh the soul thrive and the fragrances of holiness are quickening the heart of man. Favor is perfect and bounty is overflowing—the doors of prosperity are opened and hearts are expanded and dilated. The drops of the cloud of favor are continually (falling) and the lakes of graces are successively overflowing. The wine of the love of God is circulating, and the melodies of thankful birds are astonishing all people distant and near.

Tablets of 'Abdu'l-Bahá 'Abbás, vol. 2

O my God! O my God! I ask thee to protect these two birds in the orchard of Thy mercy, confirmed in joy and happiness in the garden of Thy bounties, warbling with the best melodies in the wood (garden) of Thy knowledge. Verily Thou art the Precious, the Mighty, the Protecting!

Tablets of 'Abdu'l-Bahá 'Abbás, vol. 1

O ye friends of mine! Illuminate the meeting with the light of the love of God, make it joyful and happy through the melody of the Kingdom of holiness, and with heavenly food and through the "Lord's Supper"[16] confer life.

Tablets of 'Abdu'l-Bahá 'Abbás, vol. 1

---

16 A term synonymous with heavenly food

I desire for you all that you will have this great assistance and partake of this great bounty, and that in spirit and heart you will strive and endeavor until the world of war become the world of peace; the world of darkness the world of light; satanic conduct be turned into heavenly behavior; the ruined places become built up; the sword be turned into the olive branch; the flash of hatred become the flame of the love of God and the noise of the gun the voice of the Kingdom; the soldiers of death the soldiers of life; all the nations of the world one nation; all races as one race; and all national anthems harmonized into one melody.

Then this material realm will be Paradise, the earth Heaven, and the world of Satan become the world of Angels.
Tablets of 'Abdu'l-Bahá 'Abbás, vol. 1

Now, through the aid and bounty of God, this power of guidance and this merciful bestowal are found in thee. Arise, therefore, in the utmost Power that thou mayest bestow spirit upon mouldering bones, give sight to the blind, balm and freshness to the depressed, and liveliness and grace to the dispirited. Every lamp will eventually be extinguished save the lamp of the Kingdom, which increaseth day by day in splendour. Every call shall ultimately weaken except the call to the Kingdom of God, which day unto day is raised. Every path shall finally be twisted except the road of the Kingdom, which straighteneth day by day. Undoubtedly heavenly melody is not to be measured with an earthly one, and artificial lights are not to be compared with the heavenly Sun. Hence one must exert endeavour in whatever is lasting and permanent so that one may more and more be illumined, strengthened and revived ...
Selections From the Writings of 'Abdu'l-Bahá.

The third station is that of the divine appearance and heavenly splendor: it is the Word of God, the Eternal Bounty, the Holy Spirit. It has neither beginning nor end, for these things are related to the world of contingencies and not to the divine world. For God the end is the same thing as the beginning. So the reckoning of days, weeks, months and years, of yesterday and today, is connected with the terrestrial globe; but in the sun there is no such thing—there is neither yesterday, today nor tomorrow, neither months nor years: all are equal. In the same way the Word of God is purified from all these conditions and is exempt from the boundaries, the laws and the limits of the world of contingency. Therefore, the reality of prophethood, which is the Word of God and the perfect state of manifestation, did not have any beginning and will not have any end; its rising is different from all others and is like that of the sun. For example, its dawning in the sign of Christ was with the utmost splendor and radiance, and this is eternal and everlasting. See how many conquering kings there have been, how many statesmen and princes, powerful organizers, all of whom have disappeared, whereas the breezes of Christ are still blowing; His light is still shining; His melody is still resounding; His standard is still waving; His armies are still fighting; His heavenly voice is still sweetly melodious; His clouds are still showering gems; His lightning is still flashing; His reflection is still clear and brilliant; His splendor is still radiating and luminous; and it is the same with those souls who are under His protection and are shining with His light.
Some Answered Questions

But these ill-omened owls have done a wrong,
    And learned to sing as the white falcon sings.
    And what of Sheba's message that the lapwing brings
    If the bittern learn to sing the lapwing's song?[17]
The Secret of Divine Civilization

---

17 Cf. Qur'án 27:20 ff

If for example a spiritually learned Muslim is conducting a debate with a Christian and he knows nothing of the glorious melodies of the Gospel, he will, no matter how much he imparts of the Qur'án and its truths, be unable to convince the Christian, and his words will fall on deaf ears. Should, however, the Christian observe that the Muslim is better versed in the fundamentals of Christianity than the Christian priests themselves, and understands the purport of the Scriptures even better than they, he will gladly accept the Muslim's arguments, and he would indeed have no other recourse.

The Secret of Divine Civilization

When for the second time the unmistakable signs of Israel's disintegration, abasement, subjection and annihilation had become apparent, then the sweet and holy breathings of the Spirit of God (Jesus) were shed across Jordan and the land of Galilee; the cloud of Divine pity overspread those skies, and rained down the copious waters of the spirit, and after those swelling showers that came from the most great Sea, the Holy Land put forth its perfume and blossomed with the knowledge of God. Then the solemn Gospel song rose up till it rang in the ears of those who dwell in the chambers of heaven, and at the touch of Jesus' breath the unmindful dead that lay in the graves of their ignorance lifted up their heads to receive eternal life.

The Secret of Divine Civilization

O Breakwell, O my dear one!

Thy song is even as birdsong now, thou pourest forth verses as to the mercy of thy Lord; of Him Who forgiveth ever, thou wert a thankful servant, wherefore hast thou entered into exceeding bliss.

Selections from the Writings of 'Abdu'l-Bahá

O my dearly beloved, O Breakwell! Thou hast been a divine bird and, forsaking thy earthly nest, thou hast soared toward the holy rose-garden of the Divine Kingdom and obtained a luminous station there!

O my dearly beloved, O Breakwell! Verily thou art like unto the birds, chanting the verses of thy Lord, the Forgiving, for thou wert a thankful servant; therefore thou hast entered (into the realm beyond) with joy and happiness!

Selections from the Writings of 'Abdu'l-Bahá

In flower-spangled meadows hath the divine springtime pitched its tents, and the spiritual are inhaling sweet scents from the Sheba of the spirit, carried their way by the east wind. Now doth the mystic nightingale carol its odes, and buds of inner meaning are bursting into blossoms delicate and fair. The field larks are become the festival's musicians, and lifting wondrous voices they cry and sing to the melodies of the Company on high, 'Blessed are ye! Glad Tidings! Glad Tidings!' And they urge on the revellers of the Abhá Paradise to drink their fill, and they eloquently hold forth upon the celestial tree, and utter their sacred cries. All this, that withered souls who tread the desert of the heedless, and faded ones lost in the sands of unconcern, may come to throbbing life again, and present themselves at the feasts and revels of the Lord God.

Selections from the Writings of 'Abdu'l-Bahá

Praise be to God, that thou hast become especialized with Divine Favor and Bounty. Thou didst become awake, beheld the lights and harkened unto the Melody of the Supreme Concourse.

Japan Will Turn Ablaze!

O ye beloved of God! Know ye, verily, that the happiness of mankind lieth in the unity and the harmony of the human race, and that spiritual and material developments are conditioned upon love and amity among all men. Consider ye the living creatures, namely those which move upon the earth and those which fly, those which graze and those which devour. Among the beasts of prey each kind liveth apart from other species of its genus, observing complete antagonism and hostility; and whenever they meet they immediately fight and draw blood, gnashing their teeth and baring their claws. This is the way in which ferocious beasts and bloodthirsty wolves behave, carnivorous animals that live by themselves and fight for their lives. But the docile, good-natured and gentle animals, whether they belong to the flying or grazing species, associate with one another in complete affinity, united in their flocks, and living their lives with enjoyment, happiness and contentment. Such are the birds that are satisfied with and grateful for a few grains; they live in complete gladness, and break into rich and melodious song while soaring over meadows, plains, hills and mountains.

The Secret of Divine Civilization

In this divine garden, thousands of fresh and verdant trees have raised their tops to the Supreme Apex and on every tree there are thousands of nests. Therefore, for thee, who art a bird of high flight, a nest has been prepared. Then soar, that thou mayest attain to that nest. This is a divine nest in the Heavenly Kingdom. Every bird that attained to this nest learned a melody and also taught the birds of the meadows the divine harmony which moves and enraptures the East and the West. Do thou therefore strive with all thy heart and soul that thou mayest abide in this nest and thrive till eternity.

Japan Will Turn Ablaze!

For instance, in Írán the fire of revolution blazed in such wise that all communities, government and nations, became afflicted with the most severe trials; but the power of the Covenant protected the Bahá'í friends to such a degree that in this turbulent storm no dust fell upon them, except in one locality, which became the cause of the spreading of the Religion of God and the diffusion of the Word of God. Now all the parties in Írán are wondering how the people of Bahá were guarded and protected. Praise be to God that in Ṭihrán and all the provinces of Írán the Call of God has been raised, the Ensign of the Covenant has been unfurled, the cry of "Yá-Bahá'u'l-Abhá!" has been heard and the melody of the Kingdom of Abhá has been promulgated among the people of intelligence ...

Bahá'í World Faith

All is to be yielded up, save only the remembrance of God; all is to be dispraised, except His praise. Today, to this melody of the Company on high, the world will leap and dance: 'Glory be to my Lord, the All-Glorious!' But know ye this: save for this song of God, no song will stir the world, and save for this nightingale-cry of truth from the Garden of God, no melody will lure away the heart. 'Whence cometh this Singer Who speaketh the Beloved's name?'

Selections from the Writings of 'Abdu'l-Bahá

This is a blessed meeting, for these revered souls have come together in complete unity and with an intelligent purpose. It is an occasion of great joy to me. Before me are faces radiant with the glad tidings of God, hearts aglow with the fire of the love of God, ears attuned to the melodies of the Kingdom and eyes illumined by the signs and evidences of Divinity.

The Promulgation of Universal Peace

Behold how the sun shines upon all creation, but only surfaces that are pure and polished can reflect its glory and light. The darkened soul has no portion of the revelation of the glorious effulgence of reality; and the soil of self, unable to take advantage of that light, does not produce growth. The eyes of the blind cannot behold the rays of the sun; only pure eyes with sound and perfect sight can receive them. Green and living trees can absorb the bounty of the sun; dead roots and withered branches are destroyed by it. Therefore, man must seek capacity and develop readiness. As long as he lacks susceptibility to divine influences, he is incapable of reflecting the light and assimilating its benefits. Sterile soil will produce nothing, even if the cloud of mercy pours rain upon it a thousand years. We must make the soil of our hearts receptive and fertile by tilling in order that the rain of divine mercy may refresh them and bring forth roses and hyacinths of heavenly planting. We must have perceiving eyes in order to see the light of the sun. We must cleanse the nostril in order to scent the fragrances of the divine rose garden. We must render the ears attentive in order to hear the summons of the supreme Kingdom. No matter how beautiful the melody, the ear that is deaf cannot hear it, cannot receive the call of the Supreme Concourse. The nostril that is clogged with dust cannot inhale the fragrant odors of the blossoms. Therefore, we must ever strive for capacity and seek readiness. As long as we lack susceptibility, the beauties and bounties of God cannot penetrate. Christ spoke a parable in which He said His words were like the seeds of the sower; some fall upon stony ground, some upon sterile soil, some are choked by thorns and thistles, but some fall upon the ready, receptive and fertile ground of human hearts. When seeds are cast upon sterile soil, no growth follows. Those cast upon stony ground will grow a short time, but lacking deep roots will wither away. Thorns and thistles destroy others completely, but the seed cast in good ground brings forth harvest and fruitage.

The Promulgation of Universal Peace

The lights of the divine traces are manifest in Palestine. The majority of the Israelitish Prophets raised the call of the Kingdom of God in this holy ground. Having spread the spiritual teachings, the nostrils of the spiritually-minded ones became fragrant, the eyes of the illumined souls became brightened, the ears were thrilled through this song, the hearts obtained eternal life from the soul-refreshing breeze of the Kingdom of God and gained supreme illumination from the splendor of the Sun of Reality. Then from this region the light was spread to Europe, America, Asia, Africa and Australia.
Tablets of the Divine Plan

O thou daughter of the Kingdom! Thy letter was received. It was like the melody of the divine nightingale, whose song delighteth the hearts. This is because its contents indicated faith, assurance and firmness in the Covenant and the Testament. Today the dynamic power of the world of existence is the power of the Covenant which like unto an artery pulsateth in the body of the contingent world and protecteth Bahá'í unity.
Selections from the Writings of 'Abdu'l-Bahá

O ye friends of God! Exert ye with heart and soul, so that association, love, unity and agreement be obtained between the hearts, all the aims may be merged into one aim, all the songs become one song and the power of the Holy Spirit may become so overwhelmingly victorious as to overcome all the forces of the world of nature. Exert yourselves; your mission is unspeakably glorious. Should success crown your enterprise, America will assuredly evolve into a center from which waves of spiritual power will emanate, and the throne of the Kingdom of God will, in the plentitude of its majesty and glory, be firmly established.
Tablets of the Divine Plan

Oh, how I yearn to see the friends united, even as a shining strand of pearls, as the brilliant Pleiades, as the rays of the sun, the gazelles of one meadow!

The mystic nightingale is singing for them; will they not listen? The bird of paradise is warbling; will they not hear? The Angel of the Kingdom of Abhá is calling to them; will they not hearken? The Messenger of the Covenant is pleading; will they not heed?

Ah! I am waiting, waiting to hear the glad news that the believers are the embodiment of sincerity and loyalty, the incarnation of love and amity and the manifestation of unity and concord!

Will they not rejoice my heart? Will they not satisfy my yearnings? Will they not heed my pleadings? will they not fulfill my hopes? Will they not answer my call?

I am waiting, I am patiently waiting!

Cited in Bahá'u'lláh and the New Era

Remember when the holy breaths of the Spirit of God (Jesus) were shedding their sweetness over Palestine and Galilee, over the shores of Jordan and the regions around Jerusalem, and the wondrous melodies of the Gospel were sounding in the ears of the spiritually illumined, all the peoples of Asia and Europe, of Africa and America, of Oceania, which comprises the islands and archipelagoes of the Pacific and Indian Oceans, were fire-worshipers and pagans, ignorant of the Divine Voice that spoke out on the Day of the Covenant. Alone the Jews believed in the divinity and oneness of God.

The Secret of Divine Civilization

Erelong our days shall draw to a close, and the birds of the meadows shall carol the anthem of departure.

Light of the World

Again, there are those famed and accomplished men of learning, possessed of praiseworthy qualities and vast erudition, who lay hold on the strong handle of the fear of God and keep to the ways of salvation. In the mirror of their minds the forms of transcendent realities are reflected, and the lamp of their inner vision derives its light from the sun of universal knowledge. They are busy by night and by day with meticulous research into such sciences as are profitable to mankind, and they devote themselves to the training of students of capacity. It is certain that to their discerning taste, the proffered treasures of kings would not compare with a single drop of the waters of knowledge, and mountains of gold and silver could not outweigh the successful solution of a difficult problem. To them, the delights that lie outside their work are only toys for children, and the cumbersome load of unnecessary possessions is only good for the ignorant and base. Content, like the birds, they give thanks for a handful of seeds, and the song of their wisdom dazzles the minds of the world's most wise.

The Secret of Divine Civilization

The West has always received spiritual enlightenment from the East. The Song of the Kingdom is first heard in the East, but in the West the greater volume of sound bursts upon the listening ears.

The Lord Christ arose as a bright Star in the Eastern sky, but the light of His Teaching shone more perfectly in the West, where His influence has taken root more firmly and His Cause has spread to a greater degree than in the land of His birth.

The sound of the Song of Christ has echoed over all the lands of the Western World and entered the hearts of its people.

Paris Talks

From the Prayers of 'Abdu'l-Bahá

Let us pray to God that He will exhilarate our spirits so we may behold the descent of His bounties, illumine our eyes to witness His great guidance and attune our ears to enjoy the celestial melodies of the heavenly Word. This is our greatest hope. This is our ultimate purpose.

The Promulgation of Universal Peace

O LORD, my God! Praise and thanksgiving be unto Thee for Thou hast guided me to the highway of the kingdom, suffered me to walk in this straight and far-stretching path, illumined my eye by beholding the splendors of Thy light, inclined my ear to the melodies of the birds of holiness from the kingdom of mysteries and attracted my heart with Thy love among the righteous.

Tablets of the Divine Plan

Lord! Do Thou kindle in their hearts the flame of Thy divine attraction and grant that the bird of love and understanding may sing within their hearts. Grant that they may be even as potent signs, resplendent standards, and perfect as Thy Word. Exalt by them Thy Cause, unfurl Thy banners and publish far and wide Thy wonders. Make by them Thy Word triumphant, and strengthen the loins of Thy loved ones. Unloose their tongues to laud Thy Name, and inspire them to do Thy holy will and pleasure. Illumine their faces in Thy Kingdom of holiness, and perfect their joy by aiding them to arise for the triumph of Thy Cause.

Bahá'í Prayers

O Thou kind Father, God! Gladden our hearts through the fragrance of Thy love. Brighten our eyes through the Light of Thy Guidance. Delight our ears with the melody of Thy Word, and shelter us all in the Stronghold of Thy Providence.

Bahá'í Prayers

O Thou kind Lord! Thou hast created all humanity from the same stock. Thou hast decreed that all shall belong to the same household. In Thy Holy Presence they are all Thy servants, and all mankind are sheltered beneath Thy Tabernacle; all have gathered together at Thy Table of Bounty; all are illumined through the light of Thy Providence.

O God! Thou art kind to all, Thou hast provided for all, dost shelter all, conferrest life upon all. Thou hast endowed each and all with talents and faculties, and all are submerged in the Ocean of Thy Mercy.

O Thou kind Lord! Unite all. Let the religions agree and make the nations one, so that they may see each other as one family and the whole earth as one home. May they all live together in perfect harmony.

O God! Raise aloft the banner of the oneness of mankind.

O God! Establish the Most Great Peace.

Cement Thou, O God, the hearts together.

O Thou kind Father, God! Gladden our hearts through the fragrance of Thy love. Brighten our eyes through the Light of Thy Guidance. Delight our ears with the melody of Thy Word, and shelter us all in the Stronghold of Thy Providence.

Thou art the Mighty and Powerful, Thou art the Forgiving and Thou art the One Who overlooketh the shortcomings of all mankind.

The Promulgation of Universal Peace

O Thou who attractest the hearts of the righteous by the magnet of favors, unto the Kingdom of El-Abha! O my Lord! Cause me to speak Thy praise, illumine my sight through the light of Thy knowledge, cause me to hear Thy Call, and quicken me with the spirit of Thy grace. Make me rejoiced at the melodies of the birds of Thy holiness, and make me a servant to Thy maid-servants.

Tablets of 'Abdu'l-Bahá 'Abbás, vol. 3

MELODIES OF LOVE
& PRAISE

From the Writings of Bahá'u'lláh

Recite ye the verses of God every morn and eventide. Whoso faileth to recite them hath not been faithful to the Covenant of God and His Testament, and whoso turneth away from these holy verses in this Day is of those who throughout eternity have turned away from God. Fear ye God,

The Kitáb-i-Aqdas

They who recite the verses of the All-Merciful in the most melodious of tones will perceive in them that with which the sovereignty of earth and heaven can never be compared. From them they will inhale the divine fragrance of My worlds—worlds which today none can discern save those who have been endowed with vision through this sublime, this beauteous Revelation. Say: These verses draw hearts that are pure unto those spiritual worlds that can neither be expressed in words nor intimated by allusion. Blessed be those who hearken.

The Kitáb-i-Aqdas

We have made it lawful for you to listen to music and singing. Take heed, however, lest listening thereto should cause you to overstep the bounds of propriety and dignity. Let your joy be the joy born of My Most Great Name, a Name that bringeth rapture to the heart, and filleth with ecstasy the minds of all who have drawn nigh unto God. We, verily, have made music as a ladder for your souls, a means whereby they may be lifted up unto the realm on high; make it not, therefore, as wings to self and passion. Truly, We are loath to see you numbered with the foolish.

The Kitáb-i-Aqdas

Blessed is the spot wherein the anthem of His praise is raised, and blessed the ear that hearkeneth unto that which hath been sent down from the heaven of the loving-kindness of thy Lord, the All-Merciful.

Tablets of Bahá'u'lláh Revealed After the Kitáb-i-Aqdas

Intone, O My servant, the verses of God that have been received by thee, as intoned by them who have drawn nigh unto Him, that the sweetness of thy melody may kindle thine own soul, and attract the hearts of all men. Whoso reciteth, in the privacy of his chamber, the verses revealed by God, the scattering angels of the Almighty shall scatter abroad the fragrance of the words uttered by his mouth, and shall cause the heart of every righteous man to throb. Though he may, at first, remain unaware of its effect, yet the virtue of the grace vouchsafed unto him must needs sooner or later exercise its influence upon his soul. Thus have the mysteries of the Revelation of God been decreed by virtue of the Will of Him Who is the Source of power and wisdom.

Gleanings from the Writings of Bahá'u'lláh

Magnified art Thou, O Lord my God! I ask Thee by Thy Name which Thou hast set up above all other names, through which the veil of heaven hath been split asunder and the Day-Star of Thy beauty hath risen above the horizon, shining with the brightness of Thy Name, the Exalted, the Most High, to succor me with Thy wondrous help and to preserve me in the shelter of Thy care and protection.

I am one of Thy handmaidens, O my Lord! Unto Thee have I turned, and in Thee have I placed my trust. Grant that I may be so confirmed in my love for Thee, and in fulfilling that which is well-pleasing unto Thee, that neither the defection of the infidels among Thy people, nor the clamor of the hypocrites among Thy creatures, may avail to keep me back from Thee.

Purge Thou mine ear, O my Lord, that I may hearken unto the verses sent down unto Thee, and illuminate my heart with the light of Thy knowledge, and loose my tongue that it may make mention of Thee and sing Thy praise. By Thy might, O my God! My soul is wedded to none beside Thee, and my heart seeketh none except Thine own Self.

No God is there beside Thee, the All-Glorious, the Great Giver, the Forgiving, the Compassionate.

Prayers and Meditations by Bahá'u'lláh

Nay, all else besides these Manifestations, live by the operation of their Will, and move and have their being through the outpourings of their grace. "But for Thee, I would have not created the heavens." Nay, all in their holy presence fade into utter nothingness, and are a thing forgotten. Human tongue can never befittingly sing their praise, and human speech can never unfold their mystery.

The Kitáb-i-Íqán

Say: Step out of Thy holy chamber, O Maid of Heaven, inmate of the Exalted Paradise! Drape thyself in whatever manner pleaseth Thee in the silken Vesture of Immortality, and put on, in the name of the All-Glorious, the broidered Robe of Light. Hear, then, the sweet, the wondrous accent of the Voice that cometh from the Throne of Thy Lord, the Inaccessible, the Most High. Unveil Thy face, and manifest the beauty of the black-eyed Damsel, and suffer not the servants of God to be deprived of the light of Thy shining countenance. Grieve not if Thou hearest the sighs of the dwellers of the earth, or the voice of the lamentation of the denizens of heaven. Leave them to perish on the dust of extinction. Let them be reduced to nothingness, inasmuch as the flame of hatred hath been kindled within their breasts. Intone, then, before the face of the peoples of earth and heaven, and in a most melodious voice, the anthem of praise, for a remembrance of Him Who is the King of the names and attributes of God. Thus have We decreed Thy destiny. Well able are We to achieve Our purpose.

Gleanings from the Writings of Bahá'u'lláh

O Pen of the Most High! Say: O people of the world! We have enjoined upon you fasting during a brief period, and at its close have designated for you Naw-Rúz as a feast. Thus hath the Day-Star of Utterance shone forth above the horizon of the Book as decreed by Him Who is the Lord of the beginning and the end. Let the days in excess of the months be placed before the month of fasting. We have ordained that these, amid all nights and days, shall be the manifestations of the letter Há, and thus they have not been bounded by the limits of the year and its months. It behoveth the people of Bahá, throughout these days, to provide good cheer for themselves, their kindred and, beyond them, the poor and needy, and with joy and exultation to hail and glorify their Lord, to sing His praise and magnify His Name ...

The Kitáb-i-Aqdas

All-praise be to Thee, O Lord, my God! I know not how to sing Thy praise, how to describe Thy glory, how to call upon Thy Name.

Prayers and Meditations by Bahá'u'lláh

Say: O my Lord, my Best-Beloved, the Mover of my actions, the Lode Star of my soul, the Voice that crieth in mine inmost being, the Object of mine heart's adoration! Praise be to Thee for having enabled me to turn my face towards Thee, for having set my soul ablaze through remembrance of Thee, for having aided Me to proclaim Thy Name and to sing Thy praises.

Gleanings from the Writings of Bahá'u'lláh

Praise be to God, the All-Possessing, the King of incomparable glory, a praise which is immeasurably above the understanding of all created things, and is exalted beyond the grasp of the minds of men. None else besides Him hath ever been able to sing adequately His praise, nor will any man succeed at any time in describing the full measure of His glory.

Gleanings from the Writings of Bahá'u'lláh

This is the Day whereon the unseen world crieth out, 'Great is thy blessedness, O earth, for thou hast been made the footstool of thy God, and been chosen as the seat of His mighty throne.'" "The world of being shineth, in this Day, with the resplendency of this Divine Revelation. All created things extol its saving grace, and sing its praises. The universe is wrapt in an ecstasy of joy and gladness ..."

Cited in The Advent of Divine Justice

The songs which the bird of thine heart had uttered in its great love for its friends have reached their ears, and moved Me to answer thy questions ...

Gleanings from the Writings of Bahá'u'lláh

I ask Thee then, O my God, by Thy light which hath illuminated all beings, and by Thy glory which hath irradiated the whole of creation, to remember Thy servant who hath been designated "Jím" in the realms of Thine eternity and the canopy of Thy grandeur. Cause him then, O my God, to hearken unto the holy melodies of Thy tender mercy, that they may draw him away from himself and from whatsoever is not of Thee, and attract him unto the dawning splendours of Thy love and adoration. Potent art Thou to accomplish this through Thy transcendent might.

Additional Prayers Revealed by Bahá'u'lláh

I entreat Thee, moreover, O Lord of all being and Possessor of all things visible and invisible, to bestow upon me a righteous child who may make mention of Thee on Thine earth and sing Thy praise throughout Thy realms; this, notwithstanding that Thou hast, with this Tablet, made me rich enough to dispense with every fruit, trace, or mention. I close my supplication, at this moment, with that which one of Thy chosen ones hath aforetime spoken: "O my Lord, leave me not childless, even though there is no better heir than Thyself."

Additional Prayers Revealed by Bahá'u'lláh

From the Writings of 'Abdu'l-Bahá

Thou kind Lord! Bestow heavenly confirmation upon this daughter of the kingdom, and graciously aid her that she may remain firm and steadfast in Thy Cause and that she may, even as a nightingale of the rose garden of mysteries, warble melodies in the Abhá Kingdom in the most wondrous tones, thereby bringing happiness to everyone. Make her exalted among the daughters of the kingdom and enable her to attain life eternal.

Thou art the Bestower, the All-Loving.

Bahá'í Prayers and Tablets for Children

O Lord my God, my Haven and my Refuge! How can I befittingly make mention of Thee, even with the most wondrous words of glorification or the most eloquent odes of praise, O Thou Almighty and Forgiving One, aware as I am that the tongue of every eloquent speaker doth falter, and every expression of praise from either human pen or tongue is confounded in its attempt to glorify but one of the signs of Thine omnipotent power or to extol a single Word that hath been created by Thee.

Twenty-six Prayers Revealed by 'Abdu'l Bahá

O Divine Providence, O forgiving Lord! How can I ever befittingly sing Thy praise or sufficiently worship and glorify Thee? Thy description by any tongue is naught but error, and Thy depiction by any pen is an evidence of folly in attempting this formidable task. The tongue is but an instrument composed of elements; voice and speech are naught but accidental attributes. How, then, can I celebrate, with the instrument of an earthly voice, the praise of Him Who hath neither peer nor likeness?

Twenty-six Prayers Revealed by 'Abdu'l Bahá

O thou bird of pleasing tones!

Thy little book of poems, which were very sweet, was read. It was a source of joy, for it was a spiritual anthem and a melody of the love of God.

Continue as long as thou canst this melody in the gatherings of the beloved; thus may the minds find rest and joy and become in tune with the love of God. When eloquence of expression, beauty of sense and sweetness of composition unite with new melodies the effect is very great, especially if it be the anthem of the verses of oneness and the songs of praise to the Lord of Glory.

Endeavor your utmost to compose beautiful poems to be chanted with heavenly music; thus may their beauty affect the minds and impress the hearts of those who listen.

Tablets of 'Abdu'l-Bahá 'Abbás, vol. 1

The Faith of the Blessed Beauty is summoning mankind to safety and love, to amity and peace; it hath raised up its tabernacle on the heights of the earth, and directeth its call to all nations. Wherefore, O ye who are God's lovers, know ye the value of this precious Faith, obey its teachings, walk in this road that is drawn straight, and show ye this way to the people. Lift up your voices and sing out the song of the Kingdom. Spread far and wide the precepts and counsels of the loving Lord, so that this world will change into another world, and this darksome earth will be flooded with light, and the dead body of mankind will arise and live; so that every soul will ask for immortality, through the holy breaths of God.

Selections from the Writings of 'Abdu'l-Bahá

Even as two birds they should warble melodies upon the branches of the tree of fellowship and harmony.

Cited in Family Life (compilation)

O ye sons and daughters of the Kingdom! Thankful, the birds of the spirit seek only to fly in the high heavens and to sing out their songs with wondrous art.

Selections from the Writings of 'Abdu'l-Bahá

This wonderful age has rent asunder the veils of superstition and has condemned the prejudice of the people of the East. Among some of the nations of the Orient, music and harmony was not approved of, but the Manifested Light, Bahá'u'lláh, in this glorious period has revealed in Holy Tablets that singing and music are the spiritual food of the hearts and souls. In this dispensation, music is one of the arts that is highly approved and is considered to be the cause of the exaltation of sad and desponding hearts.

Therefore ... set to music the verses and the divine words so that they may be sung with soul-stirring melody in the Assemblies and gatherings, and that the hearts of the listeners may become tumultuous and rise towards the Kingdom of Abhá in supplication and prayer.

Bahá'í World Faith

O my God! O my God! Thou seest these children who are the twigs of the tree of life, the birds of the meads of salvation, the pearls of the ocean of Thy grace, the roses of the garden of Thy guidance.

O God, our Lord! We sing Thy praise, bear witness to Thy sanctity and implore fervently the heaven of Thy mercy to make us lights of guidance, stars shining above the horizons of eternal glory amongst mankind, and to teach us a knowledge which proceedeth from Thee. Yá Bahá'u'l-Abhá!

Bahá'í Prayers and Tablets for Children

The Ancient Beauty, the Most Great Name, tasted the poison of every tribulation and quaffed from the brimming cup of every bitter affliction. He made His breast the target of every dart and readied His neck to every sword. He was cast into prison and bound by pitiless chains. He was beset by ferocious foes and attacked with stones hurled by the wicked. He was subjected to chains and fetters and confined to shackles and stocks. He was exiled from His homeland, banished to the lands of the Bulgars and the Serbs, and finally sore tried by grave affliction in the Most Great Prison. In this darksome pit, this prison of tyranny, His blessed days came to an end and He winged His flight to His Kingdom.

And now, O faithful friends, O loved ones of that luminous Beauty! Would it be meet and seemly for us to rest even for a moment? Would it be fitting for us to tarry or delay, to seek our own ease or comfort, thereby falling prey to idleness and tests, becoming preoccupied with our own fancies, and setting our affections on friend and stranger alike? Nay, by God! It behoveth us not to rest for a moment, whether by day or by night, nor to defile our pure hearts with the corruption of this world. We must spread a banquet of renunciation; hold a festival of love; lift up our voices and sing the blissful anthems of the Abhá Kingdom to the melody of the harp, the tambour, and the flute; and, hastening with joy and rapture to the field of martyrdom, surrender our lives and our all in His path.

Light of the World

The teacher, when teaching, must be himself fully enkindled, so that his utterance, like unto a flame of fire, may exert influence and consume the veil of self and passion. He must also be utterly humble and lowly so that others may be edified, and be totally self-effaced and evanescent so that he may teach with the melody of the Concourse on high—otherwise his teaching will have no effect.

Selections from the Writings of 'Abdu'l-Bahá

Praise be to Him! The renown of His Cause hath reached to east and west, and word of the power of the Abhá Beauty hath quickened north and south. That cry from the American continent is a choir of holiness, that shout from far and near that riseth even to the Company on high is 'Yá Bahá'u'l-Abhá!' Now is the east lit up with a glory, and the west rose-sweet, and all the earth is fragrant with ambergris, and the winds that blow over the Holy Shrine are laden with musk. Erelong shall ye see that even the darkest lands are bright, and the continents of Europe and Africa have turned into gardens of flowers, and forests of blossoming trees.

Selections from the Writings of 'Abdu'l-Bahá

As to thy stay in the Murgh-Mahallih[1] of Shimírán for a change of air, this is truly a divine favour That place is not the abode of mere birds, but the nest of the Phoenix of the East and the dwelling of the mystic Bird of the sacred Mount. For there, in that pure and hallowed field, the Blessed Beauty—may my life be offered up for His loved ones—took up residence for an entire summer. There he resided in the garden of Ḥájí-Báqir, which consisted of three terraces overlooking a lake. This was in the earliest days of the Cause, when that district became the throne of the Lord of the Kingdom. A large stone platform was raised in the heart of the lake, with a tent in the centre and gardens all around. About one hundred and fifty friends would gather, and at night hymns of praise would rise up to the Concourse on high. Those were wonderful times indeed. The Blessed Beauty would frequently make mention of that place.

Light of the World

---

1 Abode of the Birds

O musician of God! ... The songsters of fellowship that abide in the gardens of holiness must pour forth such a triumphant burst of songs in this age that the birds in the fields may wing their flight in a transport of delight; and in this divine festival, this heavenly banquet, they should play the lute and the harp, and the viol and the lyre in such wise that the people of east and west may be filled with exceeding joy and gladness, and be carried away with exultation and happiness.

The Importance of the Arts in Promoting the Faith (compilation)

Thy splendid letter aroused spiritual affections in my heart. I read it with admiration, for it was a melody of Divine Unity and an ensign proclaiming His oneness.

Light of the World

O thou revered maidservant of God! Thy letter from Los Angeles was received. Thank divine Providence that thou hast been assisted in service and hast been the cause of the promulgation of the oneness of the world of humanity, so that the darkness of differences among men may be dissipated, and the pavilion of the unity of nations may cast its shadow over all regions. Without such unity, rest and comfort, peace and universal reconciliation are unachievable. This illumined century needeth and calleth for its fulfilment. In every century a particular and central theme is, in accordance with the requirements of that century, confirmed by God. In this illumined age that which is confirmed is the oneness of the world of humanity. Every soul who serveth this oneness will undoubtedly be assisted and confirmed.

I hope that in the assemblies thou mayest sing praises with a sweet melody and thus become the cause of joy and gladness to all.

Selections from the Writings of 'Abdu'l-Bahá

Strive, therefore, with heart and soul that ye become ignited candles in the assemblage of the world, glittering stars on the horizon of Truth and may become the cause of the propagation of the light of the Kingdom; in order that the world of humanity may be converted into a divine realm, the nether world may become the world on high, the love of God and the mercy of the Lord may raise their canopy upon the apex of the world, human souls may become the waves of the ocean of truth, the world of humanity may grow into one blessed tree, the verses of oneness may be chanted and the melodies of sanctity may reach the Supreme Concourse.

Selections from the Writings of 'Abdu'l-Bahá

When the friends do not endeavour to spread the message, they fail to remember God befittingly, and will not witness the tokens of assistance and confirmation from the Abhá Kingdom nor comprehend the divine mysteries. However, when the tongue of the teacher is engaged in teaching, he will naturally himself be stimulated, will become a magnet attracting the divine aid and bounty of the Kingdom, and will be like unto the bird at the hour of dawn, which itself becometh exhilarated by its own singing, its warbling and its melody.

Selections from the Writings of 'Abdu'l-Bahá

O Bashír-i-Iláhí! Thy letter was like unto a treasury of poems in glorification and praise of the Blessed Beauty. It hath imparted the utmost joy and gladness. Each word of thy letter is a sign of joyous music: One word is the lyre and the lute; another, the psalms of the House of David. One word is the timbrel and the harp; another, pure poetry and song. It is a perfect symphony, causing the listeners to leap with rapture and joy. From afar thou playest the melody, and here His lovers rejoice with ecstasy.

Light of the World

Wherefore, O ye friends of God, redouble your efforts, strain every nerve, till ye triumph in your servitude to the Ancient Beauty, the Manifest Light, and become the cause of spreading far and wide the rays of the Day-Star of Truth. Breathe ye into the world's worn and wasted body the fresh breath of life, and in the furrows of every region sow ye holy seed. Rise up to champion this Cause; open your lips and teach. In the meeting place of life be ye a guiding candle; in the skies of this world be dazzling stars; in the gardens of unity be birds of the spirit, singing of inner truths and mysteries.

Selections from the Writings of 'Abdu'l-Bahá

O thou who art attracted by the Fragrances of God!

Verily, I read thy poem, which contained new significances and beautiful words. My heart was dilated by its eloquent sense. I prayed God to make thee utter more beautiful compositions that this. Thus thou mayest be the first to praise the Beauty of El-ABHA and the first utterer of His Name among the women.

Chant the verses of guidance among the people and commence [the composition of] melodies of great beauty and effect in praise and glorification of the Generous Lord ... O maid-servant of God! Warble as birds in the garden of joy and pray to thy forgiving Lord, so that the souls may rejoice through the psalms of the descendant of David.

Tablets of 'Abdu'l-Bahá 'Abbás, vol. 1

I hope thou wilt memorize all the poetry of the Blessed Perfection and chant with wonderful melody in the assemblages and gatherings. These verses will soon be translated into English poetical form and then this Divine Song will rise from those lands and reach the ABHA Kingdom in utmost joy and happiness.

Tablets of 'Abdu'l-Bahá 'Abbás, vol. 1

You have written concerning the Feast of Remembrance which you arranged after the Persian manner, at which Mr ... and Mr ... engaged in serving the beloved ones like unto Abdul-Baha: This arrangement of festivities and affection, chanting of Tablets, explaining realities and significances, and this inculcating of the teachings and exhortations of Abdul-Baha causeth everlasting life and maketh the hearers as heavenly angels ... As to chanting supplications in the Oriental tune, this is very agreeable. His honor ... must exert his endeavors in this matter.

Tablets of 'Abdu'l-Bahá 'Abbás, vol. 3

Know thou, verily, I read thy letter which expressed the commemoration of thy Lord, the Great, and indicated that the fire of the love of God is ablaze in thy heart and in the soul of the sincere ones. Truly I say unto thee, verily thy magnificent letter was as one of the melodies of the birds of holiness in the wonderful garden. Verily the hearts of the Supreme Concourse are dilated with the songs which thou hast warbled on the Blessed Tree in the Exalted Paradise ... O maid-servant of God! Be rejoiced at this glad-tidings whereby the hearts of the people of the Kingdom of El-Abha are moved with joy. Verily I beseech God to make Green Acre as the paradise of El-Abha, so that the melodies of the nightingale of sanctity may be heard from it and that the chanting of the verses of unity may be raised therein; to cause the clouds of the great gift to pour upon it the rains falling from heaven; to make those countries become verdant with the myrtles of truth and inner significances and to plant therein blessed trees, with the hand of Providence, which may bring forth pure and excellent fruits wherefrom the fragrances of God may be diffused throughout all regions. These signs shall surely appear and these lights shall shine forth.

Tablets of 'Abdu'l-Bahá 'Abbás, vol. 2

I ask God that thou mayest find rest and comfort in the shelter of the holy Banner of Peace and Concord; become the means of spreading the love of God; attain boundless health and security; grow joyfully, day by day, through the glad-tidings; soar on high through ecstasy and delight; sings the melody and proclaim the call, "Ya Baha-ul-ABHA!"

O maid-servant of God! That call to which thou didst listen is from the Kingdom of ABHA. Therefore, praise and glorify the Possessor of that Call, so that the call may be repeated.

Tablets of 'Abdu'l-Bahá 'Abbás, vol. 1

As to the difference between inspiration and imagination: Inspiration is in conformity with the Divine Texts, but imaginations do not conform therewith. A real, spiritual connection between the True One and the servant is a luminous bounty which causeth an ecstatic (or divine) flame, passion and attraction. When this connection is secured (or realized) such an ecstasy and happiness become manifest in the heart that man doth fly away (with joy) and uttereth melody and song. Just as the soul bringeth the body in motion, so that spiritual bounty and real connection likewise moveth (or cheereth) the human soul.

Tablets of 'Abdu'l-Bahá 'Abbás, vol. 1

O thou honorable one!

Thank thou God that thou art instructed in music and melody, singing with pleasant voice the glorification and praise of the Eternal, the Living. I pray to God that thou mayest employ this talent in prayer and supplication, in order that the souls may become quickened, the hearts may become attracted and all may become inflamed with the fire of the love of God!

Tablets of 'Abdu'l-Bahá 'Abbás, vol. 3

Cast behind every single thought and idea and attach thyself to the commemoration of thy Master, the Ancient. Be thou soaring in the Kingdom of God, the Mighty, the Beneficent. Live thou in Paris until the fragrance of the love of God may emanate from thee in the college wherein thou art studying sciences and unfurl thou the standard of universal peace, reconciliation, agreement and security among all men. Rejoice thou by the bounty of thy Lord which hath encompassed the whole existence and sing and warble with the most wonderful melody in the rose-garden of knowledge. Verily thy Lord, the Beneficent, will confirm thee in every moment and second and will empower thee with such a power that the columns of warfare and bloodshed shall shake and the foundation of peace and harmony shall arise.

Tablets of 'Abdu'l-Bahá 'Abbás, vol. 2

The hosts of the Kingdom of Abha are drawn and filed up in battle-array on the plain of the Supreme Apex and are expecting that a band of volunteers step upon the field of action with the intention of service; so that they may assist that band and make it victorious and triumphant.

O Thou Almighty God! Confirm Thou these friends and the maid-servants of the Merciful! Grant Thou to them assistance. Open Thou before their faces the closed doors and make them intimate with the fragrances of holiness, so that they may become the confident friends of each other; raise the melody and the song of joy and sing the harmony of heaven, in order that they may exhilarate and gladden the regions of the West and impart attraction and ecstasy!

Make Thou them the magnets of love so that they may attract the hearts to the Kingdom of Abha!

Tablets of 'Abdu'l-Bahá 'Abbás, vol. 2

His Holiness Christ, addressing the believers, uttereth the following in the Gospel: "Be awake lest the Son of Man come and find ye asleep!" Now, thou wast awake, therefore thou didst advance and engage in the service of the Word of God. Appreciate the value of this attainment, and, like unto a candle, radiate the light of the love of God in the meeting of the beloved. Encourage the beloved of God and be a source of joy and gladness to the Bahais. Hold meetings and read and chant the heavenly teachings, so that city may be illumined with the light of reality and that country become a veritable paradise by the strength of the Holy Spirit, for this cycle is the cycle of the Glorious Lord and the melody of oneness and solidarity of the world of mankind must reach the ears of the East and West.

Tablets of 'Abdu'l-Bahá 'Abbás, vol. 3

O Lord! Should the breath of the Holy Spirit confirm the weakest of creatures, he would attain all to which he aspireth and would possess anything he desireth. Indeed, Thou hast assisted Thy servants in the past and, though they were the weakest of Thy creatures, the lowliest of Thy servants and the most insignificant of those who lived upon the earth, through Thy sanction and potency they took precedence over the most glorious of Thy people and the most noble of mankind. Whereas formerly they were as moths, they became as royal falcons, and whereas before they were as brooks, they became as seas, through Thy bestowal and Thy mercy. They became, through Thy most great favor, stars shining on the horizon of guidance, birds singing in the rose gardens of immortality, lions roaring in the forests of knowledge and wisdom, and whales swimming in the oceans of life.

Tablets of the Divine Plan

Raise ye a clamour like unto a roaring sea; like a prodigal cloud, rain down the grace of heaven. Lift up your voices and sing out the songs of the Abhá Realm. Quench ye the fires of war, lift high the banners of peace, work for the oneness of humankind and remember that religion is the channel of love unto all peoples.

Selections from the Writings of 'Abdu'l-Bahá

O ye esteemed maid-servants of God, and ye revered beloved ones (or men believers) of the Merciful!

Your letter was received and its contents noted. The maid-servant of God, she who hath ascended to heaven, i.e., Mrs ... hastened from this mortal world to the divine world and soared from this temporal realm to the expanse of the Kingdom. She abandoned the earthly cage and flew toward the bower of the upper world; so that, like unto a nightingale of significances, she may, in that divine rose-garden, engage in praising, glorifying and sanctifying the True One, with the most marvelous melody.

Consequently, do ye not sigh in grief of her decease, and be not dejected on account of her ascension.

Tablets of 'Abdu'l-Bahá 'Abbás, vol. 2

Then, O ye friends of God! Appreciate the value of this precious Revelation, move and act in accordance with it and walk in the straight path and the right way. Show it to the people. Raise the melody of the Kingdom and spread abroad the teachings and ordinances of the loving Lord so that the world may become another world, the darkened earth may become illumined and the dead body of the people may obtain new life. Every soul may seek everlasting life through the breath of the Merciful.

Bahá'í World Faith

O ye beloved friends of Abdul-Baha!

The news of your spiritual assembly reached this Illumined Spot and the heart of this yearning one was rejoiced on account of your concord, unity and affinity. What wonderful meetings and brilliant gatherings were those, whose fame will become world-wide and whose melody will ere long reach to all the kingdoms! that in the region of America the believers are real companions and associates with each other and are as beloved friends among themselves; that they bring about gatherings of friendship, engage themselves in the praise and glorification of the glorious Lord, deliver eloquent speeches, establish the proofs and arguments of the Manifestation of the Sun of Truth, spread the divine teachings and shed broadcast the musk-diffusing fragrances of the Kingdom, so that the nostrils become perfumed and the eyes become brightened.

O ye friends! O ye maid-servants of the Merciful! Those assemblies are the emblems of the Supreme Concourse and the prototypes of the congregations of the spirits in the Kingdom of Abha. Avail yourselves of the opportunities of this time, neither let the occasion slip by unheeded. The season of the soul-refreshing springtime will not appear at all time, neither will the breezy dawn be at every moment. Now is the time of proclamation and the occasion of supplication and invocation toward the Kingdom of Abha.

Therefore, sing ye the sweet melody in the assemblages, entreat ye at the Threshold of the Kingdom of the Lord of Hosts and beg ye for confirmation and assistance. The Guide of Providence will appear and the "beloved of divine gift" will unveil her luminous countenance.

Tablets of 'Abdu'l-Bahá 'Abbás, vol. 3

O Divine Providence! This assemblage is composed of Thy friends who are attracted to Thy beauty and are set ablaze by the fire of Thy love. Turn these souls into heavenly angels,

resuscitate them through the breath of Thy Holy Spirit, grant them eloquent tongues and resolute hearts, bestow upon them heavenly power and merciful susceptibilities, cause them to become the promulgators of the oneness of mankind and the cause of love and concord in the world of humanity, so that the perilous darkness of ignorant prejudice may vanish through the light of the Sun of Truth, this dreary world may become illumined, this material realm may absorb the rays of the world of spirit, these different colors may merge into one color and the melody of praise may rise to the kingdom of Thy sanctity. Verily, Thou art the Omnipotent, and the Almighty!
Bahá'í Prayers

O thou worshipper of Truth!

Thy letter was received and its contents became known. Praise be to God! Immense results and great effect have been produced by forwarding [recent] Tablets to that country (America). They gladdened and exhilarated the friends and imparted happiness to the souls. They granted sight to the eyes and hearing to the ears. It is hoped that wonderful effects will be displayed in the future, that the friends of God may live and act in accord with the heavenly teachings, in order that the region of America may become the Paradise of Abha, that desert and wilderness become the rose-garden of human perfections, the verses of guidance be read, the melody of "Ya Baha El-Abha!" reach the Kingdom of Beauty; warfare and bloodshed be removed from among the people, affinity and love hoist their tent upon the apex of the world, all mankind become real friends with one another and each soul respect the other. Whenever these signs appear, then it will become manifest that the Tablets have had their effect.
Tablets of 'Abdu'l-Bahá 'Abbás, vol. 3

The following commune is to be read by them every day:

O GOD! O God! This is a broken-winged bird and his flight is very slow—assist him so that he may fly toward the apex of prosperity and salvation, wing his way with the utmost joy and happiness throughout the illimitable space, raise his melody in Thy Supreme Name in all the regions, exhilarate the ears with this call, and brighten the eyes by beholding the signs of guidance.

O Lord! I am single, alone and lowly. For me there is no support save Thee, no helper except Thee and no sustainer beside Thee. Confirm me in Thy service, assist me with the cohorts of Thine angels, make me victorious in the promotion of Thy Word and suffer me to speak out Thy wisdom amongst Thy creatures. Verily, Thou art the helper of the weak and the defender of the little ones, and verily Thou art the Powerful, the Mighty and the Unconstrained.

Tablets of the Divine Plan

The beloved of the Lord, with their musk-scented breath, burn like bright candles in every clime, and the friends of the All-Merciful, even as unfolding flowers, can be found in all regions. Not for a moment do they rest; they breathe not but in remembrance of Thee, and crave naught but to serve Thy Cause. In the meadows of truth they are as sweet-singing nightingales, and in the flower-garden of guidance they are even as brightly-coloured blossoms. With mystic flowers they adorn the walks of the Garden of Reality; as swaying cypresses they line the riverbanks of the Divine Will. Above the horizon of being they shine as radiant stars; in the firmament of the world they gleam as resplendent orbs. Manifestations of celestial grace are they, and daysprings of the light of divine assistance.

Selections from the Writings of 'Abdu'l-Bahá

Be, therefore, a divine bird, proceed to thy native country, spread the wings of sanctity over those spots and sing and chant and celebrate the name of thy Lord, that thou mayest gladden the Supreme Concourse and make the seeking souls hasten unto thee as the moths hasten to the lamp, and thus illumine that distant country by the light of God.

Tablets of 'Abdu'l-Bahá 'Abbás, vol. 2

O ye merciful friends of Abdul-Baha! At this moment a letter hath been received from America containing the good news that that region of the Occident hath become the Orient; that is, in that region the rays of the Sun of Truth have appeared and shone forth with such penetration that the bright light of the morn of guidance hath dawned and every longing one hath attained to the desire of this heart, and that the melody of the Kingdom of Abha ascends continuously to the Supreme Concourse and the soul-refreshing strains of "Ya Baha El-Abha!" reach the ears of the peoples and communities of that country.

Tablets of 'Abdu'l-Bahá 'Abbás, vol. 2

If, in this momentous task, a mighty effort be exerted, the world of humanity will shine out with other adornings, and shed the fairest light. Then will this darksome place grow luminous, and this abode of earth turn into Heaven. The very demons will change to angels then, and wolves to shepherds of the flock, and the wild-dog pack to gazelles that pasture on the plains of oneness, and ravening beasts to peaceful herds, and birds of prey, with talons sharp as knives, to songsters warbling their sweet native notes.

Selections from the Writings of 'Abdu'l-Bahá

Heroes are they, O my Lord, lead them to the field of battle. Guides are they, make them to speak out with arguments and proofs. Ministering servants are they, cause them to pass round the cup that brimmeth with the wine of certitude. O my God, make them to be songsters that carol in fair gardens, make them lions that couch in the thickets, whales that plunge in the vasty deep.

Selections from the Writings of 'Abdu'l-Bahá

Then let you engage in the praise of Bahá'u'lláh, for it is through His grace and succour that ye have become sons and daughters of the Kingdom; it is thanks to Him that ye are now songsters in the meadows of truth, and have soared upward to the heights of the glory that abideth forever. Ye have found your place in the world that dieth not; the breaths of the Holy Spirit have blown upon you; ye have taken on another life, ye have gained access to the Threshold of God.

Selections from the Writings of 'Abdu'l-Bahá

Now is the time for the lovers of God to raise high the banners of unity, to intone, in the assemblages of the world, the verses of friendship and love and to demonstrate to all that the grace of God is one. Thus will the tabernacles of holiness be upraised on the summits of the earth, gathering all peoples into the protective shadow of the Word of Oneness. This great bounty will dawn over the world at the time when the lovers of God shall arise to carry out His Teachings, and to scatter far and wide the fresh, sweet scents of universal love.

Selections from the Writings of 'Abdu'l-Bahá

Wherefore, O beloved of the Lord, strive ye with heart and soul to receive a share of His holy attributes and take your portion of the bounties of His sanctity—that ye may become the tokens of unity, the standards of singleness, and seek out the meaning of oneness; that ye may, in this garden of God, lift up your voices and sing the blissful anthems of the spirit. Become ye as the birds who offer Him their thanks, and in the blossoming bowers of life chant ye such melodies as will dazzle the minds of those who know. Raise ye a banner on the highest peaks of the world, a flag of God's favour to ripple and wave in the winds of His grace; plant ye a tree in the field of life, amid the roses of this visible world, that will yield a fruitage fresh and sweet.

Selections from the Writings of 'Abdu'l-Bahá

Therefore, O ye friends of God! Show ye forth an earnest endeavor and display ye a resolute effort, so that ye may become assisted in the adoration of the Ancient Beauty and the Manifest Light; to be the cause of spreading the light of the Sun of Truth; to infuse into the dead, antiquated body of the world a new spirit; to cast in the fields of the hearts pure seeds; to arise in the service of the Cause; to speak with eloquent tongues; to become candles of guidance in the assemblage of the world; to become shining stars in the horizon of the existent being; to become merciful birds in the rose-garden of oneness; to sing the melodies of realities and significances; to spend every breath of your lives in the most great Cause; and to devote the period of your existence to the service of this conspicuous Light; so that in the end ye may be freed from loss and failure and attain to the inexhaustible treasury of the Kingdom.

Tablets of 'Abdu'l-Bahá 'Abbás, vol. 3

'Abdu'l-Bahá's supreme joy is in observing that a number of leaves from among the handmaidens of the Blessed Beauty have been educated, that they are the essence of detachment, and are well-informed of the mysteries of the world of being; that they raise such a call in their glorification and praise of the Greatest Name as to cause the inmates of the Fanes of the Kingdom to become attracted and overjoyed, and that they recite prayers in prose and poetry, and melodiously chant the divine verses. I cherish the hope that thou wilt be one of them, wilt cast forth pearls, wilt be constantly engaged in singing His praise and wilt intone celestial strains in glorification of His attributes ...

Women (compilation)

The time hath come when, as a thank-offering for this bestowal, ye should grow in faith and constancy as day followeth day, and should draw ever nearer to the Lord, your God, becoming magnetized to such a degree, and so aflame, that your holy melodies in praise of the Beloved will reach upward to the Company on high; and that each one of you, even as a nightingale in this rose garden of God, will glorify the Lord of Hosts, and become the teacher of all who dwell on earth.

Selections from the Writings of 'Abdu'l-Bahá

Take the cup of sanctity in thy right hand and pass the glass of the Kingdom, in the social meeting—which is the wine of the love of God and the sweet, pure, cool water of the knowledge of God—and give to drink to those who are in attendance, that they may rejoice, be happy and sing the hymns of sanctity and unification, offering their praise to the Supreme Kingdom.

Tablets of 'Abdu'l-Bahá 'Abbás, vol. 1

Bestow upon them the everlasting life and bless them with the new teachings. Make every one a lighted torch and a warbling nightingale—the king of the rose in the garden. Reveal to them Thine attractive beauty; make each a growing tree on the shore of Thy guidance, bearing the fruit of Thy grace. Thus may the East illumine the West and the West become the East of the Supreme Heaven.

Tablets of 'Abdu'l-Bahá 'Abbás, vol. 1

Do not wonder at the favor and bounty of the Lord. By the favor of God, how often a drop hath become undulating like a sea, and an atom become shining like the sun!

The Sun of Truth hath enlightened the divine world and illumined the universe. The rays of His grace have shone upon the East and West, and His heat hath caused vegetation in all countries. So the lights and the heat of the Sun of Truth being help and assistance, what more dost thou need?

Thou must warble, like the nightingale of significances, in the rose garden so that thou mayest inspire all the birds of the meadow to chant and to sing.

Japan Will Turn Ablaze!

Therefore, roll up thy sleeves to serve the Covenant, make the hearts firm in the Covenant of the beloved Lord, create harmony and agreement among the believers and impart to them the glad-tidings of the confirmation which they will receive from God if the differences of opinion be removed and if they unite and agree, be firm in spreading the fragrance of God, divulging the traces and chanting the signs of God.

Tablets of 'Abdu'l-Bahá 'Abbás, vol. 1

As to thee, convey unto the maid-servants of the Merciful that they must be firm in the love of El-Baha at the time of the severe trials and tests; forasmuch as the storms and winds occur during the winter seasons; then comes the spring with the wonderful scenery and it adorns the hills and plains with flowers and beautiful birds sing the melodies of joy on the branches of the trees and warble beautiful tunes on the roofs of bowers, in wonderful melodies. Soon shalt thou see that the lights have shone forth, the banners of the Kingdom have been raised, the fragrances of God diffused, the hosts of the Kingdom descending, the angels of heaven confirmed and the Holy Spirit breathed into those horizons (regions). Then shalt thou see the waverers frightened and at loss. This is a complete matter on the part of the Lord of Signs.

Tablets of 'Abdu'l-Bahá 'Abbás, vol. 1

Blessed ye are, O ye pure and chaste ones! Glad-tidings be unto you through the gift of the Covenant, from the light of which all regions are illuminated! Be rejoiced that the lights of the Sun of Truth are shining forth unto all parts; be gladdened at the gifts of your Lord, which have surrounded all the universe; dilate your breasts by chanting the verses of God, and console your eyes by witnessing the bounties of the Supreme Concourse.

Tablets of 'Abdu'l-Bahá 'Abbás, vol. 1

O thou who art attracted to God!

I send this letter written by my own hand, that thou mayest thank God, thy Lord, the Supreme, grow in happiness in the love of God and be kindled by the fire of His love, chanting verses of greetings and thanks, and be quickened by the breezes of life blown from the garden of the knowledge of God.

Tablets of 'Abdu'l-Bahá 'Abbás, vol. 1

O thou who art attracted by the Fragrances of God!

Verily I read thy last letter and gathered from its meanings the mysteries of thy great love. I supplicate to my Lord that He may at every moment increase thy joy and fragrance, thy speech and utterance, thine attraction and enkindlement, and that He may heal thee from the infirmities which have affected thee and weakened thy feeble body, and strengthen thee to guide mankind into the Supreme Kingdom and quicken hearts by the fragrances of the Paradise of Abha, so that thou mayest become a bird warbling upon the twigs of the Tree of Life, with most wonderful melodies and most charming tunes.

Tablets of 'Abdu'l-Bahá 'Abbás, vol. 2

O ye friends of this prisoner!

According to what is heard and evident, you have arranged an assembly in the utmost beauty and a number of you present yourselves in that meeting with all love and unity and engage in communion (i.e., reading of the communes), chanting of the verses, spiritual conversation and utterance of the Kingdom. Blessed are ye for having adorned such a meeting and for having prepared such a feast! That gathering receiveth bounty from the Supreme Concourse and that nucleus is under the protection of the Bounty of Abha.

Tablets of 'Abdu'l-Bahá 'Abbás, vol. 3

Go out from the solitary place like unto a shining star blazing on its horizon. This is better for thee in the Kingdom of the Lord of the worlds. Thus, hearken unto the melodies of the birds of holiness, in the garden of fellowship, upon the branches of purity; to the murmuring of its waters, the rustling of the trees, the blowing of its breezes and the cooing of its doves.

Tablets of 'Abdu'l-Bahá 'Abbás, vol. 3

O my friend, verily the Cause is great and great, and the penetration of the Word of God in the temple (body) of all the regions is similar to the pervasion of the soul in a sound body.

By the life of Bahá, verily, the power of the Kingdom of God hath taken hold of the pillars of the world, and hath possessed all the nations. Thou wilt surely find the standards of the Testament waving in all regions, the chanting of the verses of unity raised in exalted assemblies, and the lights of the Sun of Truth and its heat dispersing the thick clouds massed on the horizon. Be rejoiced at this glad-tidings, whereby the hearts of the sincere among the beloved are cheered.

Tablets of 'Abdu'l-Bahá 'Abbás, vol. 1

O ye illumined faces! O ye divine souls! and O ye spiritual temples!

Verily, I read your letter which uttered your extreme love and entire attraction to the Kingdom of God, your trust in God, your immersing into the deep seas of the bounties of God and your chanting the verses of thanksgiving to God, because He guided you to His Eternal Kingdom, manifested to you His evident light, descended upon you a heavenly table through His great favor, planted you in His glorious vineyard and caused you to become manifestations of guidance among the people and dawning-points of wisdom among the creatures.

Tablets of 'Abdu'l-Bahá 'Abbás, vol. 1

O thou who art kindled as a lamp with the Fire of the Love of God!

Be thou a fountain flowing with the waters of the mercy of God, a myrtle perfumed with the fragrances of God and a bird warbling the most wonderful melodies of the knowledge of God in the garden of faith.

Tablets of 'Abdu'l-Bahá 'Abbás, vol. 2

Thus with a heavenly power, divine strength, merciful fragrance, supreme light, and conscious attraction, may they arise to serve Thee, to perfume the East and the West with the fragrances of holiness, establish the universal peace, promulgate integrity and honesty, to adore the truth, become a means of life to the people of the world, a cause of comfort and rest to them; to help the spiritual meeting, to serve the gathering of the Lord, to send well-informed souls (teachers) to other regions and climes, to be self-sacrificing with life and heart, to build the Mashrak-el-Azcar, to raise the anthem of sanctity to the Supreme Kingdom, to live in perfect love with one another ...

Tablets of 'Abdu'l-Bahá 'Abbás, vol. 2

Blessed is the pure blood which was shed on the perfumed soil, and which was poured out in the path of the forgiving Lord! Blessed is thy body which was burned by the hand of every transgressor! Blessed is thy throat which was cut by the poniard of every traitor! Blessed is thy breast which was stricken by the oppressors' darts! Blessed is thy heart which was wounded by a sharp sword! Blessed art thou, for thou hast showed forth all happiness and joy when thou wert being paraded in the streets of the people of haughtiness and the people of wickedness were clapping their hands and oppressing thee with innumerable blows and wounds, whilst thou wert clapping thy hands with them—O thou manifestor of light!—and wert warbling melodies, whereby the people of the Kingdom of El-Abha were moved and breasts dilated (with joy)!

Tablets of 'Abdu'l-Bahá 'Abbás, vol. 2

Among the people, a multitude became intoxicated with this divine wine—and a multitude were deprived of this great favor. Many a soul enlightened his sight and insight by the radiance of grace, and many were cheered and rejoiced at the melodies of unity. Some birds sang melodies and harmonies, and some nightingales began to warble on the branches of the rose-tree of mercifulness. The Kingdom and the phenomenal world were adorned, and became the envy of the delectable paradise ...

Tablets of 'Abdu'l-Bahá 'Abbás, vol. 2

O thou maid-servant of God who art attracted to the Fragrances of God!

Speak of my servitude unto God, of my humbleness and submissiveness to the Beloved of God, and of my evanescence, nothingness and utter meekness to the Threshold of Baha'. Verily, I am the servant of Baha', the slave of Baha' and the captive of Baha'. I have no grade but this and I do not possess anything for myself. Therefore, mention me in my pure servitude; this is that by which my heart is dilated by every maid-servant who speaks the praise of God. I beseech God to make thee a dove in the grove of holiness, to coo with the most wonderful melodies the praise of thy Lord, the Merciful!

Tablets of 'Abdu'l-Bahá 'Abbás, vol. 3

O thou Eternal One! Make the friends of that country prosperous, acquaint them with the mysteries; usher them into the divine rose-garden and reveal to them the hidden realities and significances; make their hearts the association of truth and their souls full of divine melodies and sacred (choral) music! O God! This respectful assemblage are my relatives and kindred and the cause of the happiness of this afflicted one. Bestow upon them a shining face and grant them a musk-diffusing character. Show them the mystery of the Kingdom and suffer them to hear the soul-elevating harmony of heaven! Awaken (the people) by the breeze of the Paradise of Abha and make them alive by the power of the Holy Spirit. Verily, Thou are the Powerful and Omnipotent, and Thou art the Bestower and generous!

Tablets of ʿAbduʾl-Bahá ʿAbbás, vol. 2

... O beloved of God, endeavor with your hearts and souls, that ye may be qualified with the morals and attributes of the Blessed Perfection, and partake of the bounties of His sanctity; that ye may become signs of unity and standards of oneness, discover the essence of singleness and sing harmonies and lays in in this divine garden, in merciful melodies; that ye may become as thankful birds, and sing a song in the rose-garden of existence which may astonish minds and senses; that ye may hoist a standard on the apex of the universe which may flutter in the winds of favor, and plant a tree in the field of the visible world which may bring forth fruits of the utmost delicacy and freshness.

Tablets of ʿAbduʾl-Bahá ʿAbbás, vol. 2

O thou son of the Kingdom! If one possesses the love of God, everything that he undertakes is useful, but if the undertaking is without the love of God, then it is hurtful and the cause of veiling one's self from the Lord of the Kingdom. But with the love of God every bitterness is changed into sweetness and every gift becometh precious. For instance, a musical and melodious voice imparteth life to an attracted heart but lureth toward lust those souls who are engulfed in passion and desire.

Tablets of ʿAbduʾl-Bahá ʿAbbás, vol. 3

Soon the whole world, as in springtime, will change its garb. The turning and falling of the autumn leaves is past; the bleakness of the winter time is over. The new year hath appeared and the spiritual springtime is at hand. The black earth is becoming a verdant garden; the deserts and mountains are teeming with red flowers; from the borders of the wilderness the tall grasses are standing like advance guards before the cypress and jessamine trees; while the birds are singing among the rose branches like the angels in the highest heavens, announcing the glad-tidings of the approach of that spiritual spring, and the sweet music of their voices is causing the real essence of all things to move and quiver.

O my spiritual friend! Dost thou know from what airs emanate the notes sung by those birds? They are from the melodies of peace and reconciliation, of love and unity, of justice and security, of concord and harmony. In a short time this heavenly singing will intoxicate all humanity; the foundations of enmity shall be destroyed; unity and affection shall be witnessed in every assembly; and the lovers of the love of God at these great festivals shall behold their splendor.

Therefore, contemplate what a spirit of life God hath given that the body of the whole earth may attain life everlasting! The Paradise of El-Abha will soon spread a pavilion from the pole-star of the world, under whose shelter the beloved shall rejoice and the pure hearts shall repose in peace.

Tablets of 'Abdu'l-Bahá 'Abbás, vol. 2

Verily, I supplicate God to enkindle in thy heart the fire of His love; and enkindlement the light of which shall affect all regions, so that thy face may become illumined by the lights of the Spirit and [give forth] fragrance in the world of possibility. Arise for the service of the Cause of God in those countries which are vast and spacious, and sing, warbling beautiful melodies in the Name of thy Lord, the Supreme.

Tablets of 'Abdu'l-Bahá 'Abbás, vol. 2

O thou chosen maid-servant of God! It is time for thee to cry aloud and fervently, day and night, not to sit still a moment, not to rest for an instant, but to be always engaged in the commemoration of God and invite the people with the utmost longing and ecstasy unto the Kingdom of God.

Raise thou such melodies and harmony in Green Acre that may reach unto the Kingdom of Abha and cause joy and exaltation in the angels of heaven! This matter needs a great enthusiasm (heat or exertion) and a sanctity and purity like unto a manifest light. Thou knowest what secrets doeth the spirit of Abdul-Baha communicate with thee and what glad-tidings he giveth unto thee! Show forth thy capacity and merit, for without capacity the Gift doth not become manifest.

Tablets of 'Abdu'l-Bahá 'Abbás, vol. 2

O thou who art attracted by the Fragrances of God! Verily, I noted thy letter and utterance. God hath accepted thy devotion, prayer and worship and hath manifested upon thee the lights of His great favor, ushered thee into His Kingdom, gave thee to drink of the wine of His love and made thee to hear the melodies of the birds of holiness in this wonderful day.

Thank God that He enriched thee beyond the delicacies of this mortal world and caused thee to taste the sweetness of His love in His New Kingdom.

O maid-servant of God! Sing with beautiful melodies in the meetings of the maid-servants, praising and glorifying thy Supreme Lord ... Confine thy interests, thy works and efforts to the Cause of God. Thus the spirit of power and might will confirm thee and the manifest light will shine upon thy brow.

Tablets of 'Abdu'l-Bahá 'Abbás, vol. 1

I hope that ye will attain the utmost patience, composure and resignation, and I entreat and implore at the Threshold of Oneness, begging for forgiveness and pardon. My hope from the infinite bounties of God is that He may shelter this dove of the garden of faith, and cause him to abide on the branch of the Supreme Concourse, that he may sing in the best of melodies the praise and glorification of the Lord of Names and Attributes.

Selections from the Writings of 'Abdu'l-Bahá

… in the states of Illinois, Wisconsin, Ohio, Michigan and Minnesota—praise be to God—believers are found who are associating with each other in the utmost firmness and steadfastness—day and night they have no other intention save the diffusion of the fragrances of God, they have no other hope except the promotion of the heavenly teachings, like the candles they are burning with the light of the love of God, and like thankful birds are singing songs, spirit-imparting, joy-creating, in the rose garden of the knowledge of God …

Tablets of the Divine Plan

O thou dear maid-servant of God!

Mr … hath greatly praised thee that—praise be to God! —thou art like unto a melodious nightingale, singing and warbling in the rose-garden of the love of God, and art uttering of the mystery of the Kingdom; that thy house and dwelling is a meeting-place of the spiritual ones and thy nest and abode is a shelter for the birds of heaven. Nothing is better than that man should become a manifestor of the powers of God and the cause of illuminating the creatures.

Tablets of 'Abdu'l-Bahá 'Abbás, vol. 3

This Feast was established by His Highness the Bab, to occur once in nineteen days. Likewise, the Blessed Perfection[2] hath commanded, encourage and reiterated it. Therefore, it hath the utmost importance. Undoubtedly you must give the greatest attention to its establishment and raise it to the highest point of importance, so that it may become continual and constant. The believers of God must assemble and associate with each other in the utmost love, joy and fragrance. They must conduct themselves (in these Feasts) with the greatest dignity and consideration, chant divine verses, peruse instructive articles, read the Tablets of Abdul-Baha, encourage and inspire each other with love for the whole human race, invoke God with perfect joy and fragrance, sing the verses, glorifications and praises of the Self-subsistent Lord and deliver eloquent speeches.

Tablets of 'Abdu'l-Bahá 'Abbás, vol. 2

O bird that singeth sweetly of the Abhá Beauty! In this new and wondrous dispensation the veils of superstition have been torn asunder and the prejudices of eastern peoples stand condemned. Among certain nations of the East, music was considered reprehensible, but in this new age the Manifest Light hath, in His holy Tablets, specifically proclaimed that music, sung or played, is spiritual food for soul and heart.

The musician's art is among those arts worthy of the highest praise, and it moveth the hearts of all who grieve. Wherefore, O thou Shahnáz,[3] play and sing out the holy words of God with wondrous tones in the gatherings of the friends, that the listener may be freed from chains of care and sorrow, and his soul may leap for joy and humble itself in prayer to the realm of Glory.

Tablets of 'Abdu'l-Bahá 'Abbás, vol. 1

---

2   Bahá'u'lláh

3   Shahnáz, the name given to the recipient of this Tablet, is also the name of a musical mode

... you must thank God that—praise be to God!—through His grace and favor the lamp of the most great guidance has been ignited in your hearts, and He has summoned you to His Kingdom. He has caused the call of the Supreme Concourse to reach your ears. The doors of heaven have been opened unto you. The Sun of Reality is shining upon you, the cloud of mercy is pouring down, and the breezes of providence are wafting through your souls. Although the bestowal is great and the grace is glorious, yet capacity and readiness are requisite. Without capacity and readiness the divine bounty will not become manifest and evident. No matter how much the cloud may rain, the sun may shine and the breezes blow, the soil that is sterile will give no growth. The ground that is pure and free from thorns and thistles receives and produces through the rain of the cloud of mercy. No matter how much the sun shines, it will have no effect upon the black rock, but in a pure and polished mirror its lights become resplendent. Therefore, we must develop capacity in order that the signs of the mercy of the Lord may be revealed in us. We must endeavor to free the soil of the hearts from useless weeds and sanctify it from the thorns of worthless thoughts in order that the cloud of mercy may bestow its power upon us. The doors of God are open, but we must be ready and fitted to enter. The ocean of divine providence is surging, but we must be able to swim. The bestowals of the Almighty are descending from the heaven of grace, but capacity to receive them is essential. The fountain of divine generosity is gushing forth, but we must have thirst for the living waters. Unless there be thirst, the salutary water will not assuage. Unless the soul hungers, the delicious foods of the heavenly table will not give sustenance. Unless the eyes of perception be opened, the lights of the sun will not be witnessed. Until the nostrils are purified, the fragrance of the divine rose garden will not be inhaled. Unless the heart be filled with longing, the favors of the Lord will not be evident. Unless a perfect melody be sung, the ears of the hearers will not be attracted. Therefore, we must endeavor night and day to purify the hearts from every dross, sanctify the souls from every restriction and become free from the discords of the human world. Then the divine bestowals will become evident in their fullness and glory. If we do not strive and sanctify ourselves from the defects and evil qualities of human nature, we will not partake of the bestowals of God. It is as if the sun is shining in its full glory, but no reflection is forthcoming from hearts that are black as stone. If an ocean of salubrious water is surging and we be not thirsty, what benefit do we receive? If the candle be lighted and we have no eyes, what enjoyment do we obtain from it? If melodious anthems should rise to the heavens and we are bereft of hearing, what enjoyment can we find?

The Promulgation of Universal Peace

O thou bird warbling in the Garden of the Love of God!

Thank God that He hath illumined thine insight, led thee unto the Fire glowing in the Tree of Man, caused thee to utter His praise among the creatures and guided certain women to whom thou delivered the Word of God ... I pray God to confirm the relatives in attaining to the Brilliant Light, to let the light of insight shine forth to the hearts and sights, to aid thy friends in being illumined by the light of El-Baha and [being] fed from the heavenly table, and to make thee empty, void from the thoughts of the life of this world and filled with the love of thy Lord, ready for His service, uttering His praise and demonstrating with proofs the appearance of the Kingdom of God.

Tablets of 'Abdu'l-Bahá 'Abbás, vol. 2

O ye two[4] singing birds in the Garden of Belief!

Tablets of 'Abdu'l-Bahá 'Abbás, vol. 2

---

4 husband and wife

O thou bird who art warbling in the Garden of the Guidance of God!

Verily, I read thy excellent and brilliant letter. It showed how thou hast sought the fire of guidance from the Sinaitic Tree, and art shining by the light of faithfulness of the Supreme Concourse.

Blessed art thou; again, blessed art thou! Glad-tidings be unto thee; again, glad-tidings be unto thee!

Appreciate the worth of this peerless and choice Pearl (of the Truth). By the life of God, verily, this is the most splendid jewel which glitters on the crown of glory, among all the people of the world.

Tablets of 'Abdu'l-Bahá 'Abbás, vol. 1

My God! My God! Elohim.

To this Thy servant give the understanding of the Old Testament and the New and enable her to speak forth with mighty voice and to sing with power the holy songs and to discover the real meaning and the secret mysteries of those verses, for Thou art the Powerful Inspirer and the Mighty One!

Tablets of 'Abdu'l-Bahá 'Abbás, vol. 2

It is incumbent upon thee to assemble continuously with the beloved of God and to meet with those whose faces are illumined with the light of the love of God. Verily, I supplicate to God to make thee sincere in this love, to illumine thee with the light of His Kingdom, and to destine unto thee the illumination by the light of His attributes, to make thee a sign of mercy, a bird warbling the verses of unity; that thou mayest be nurtured in the bosom of His providence, and become a growing tree bearing fruit in the Paradise of El-Abha.

Bahá'í World Faith

If thou art a hero of the field and a melodious bird in the garden of the Merciful One, speak of the Beauty of Abha, for it is ready and present.

Tablets of 'Abdu'l-Bahá 'Abbás, vol. 2

O thou son of the Kingdom! All things are beneficial if joined with the love of God; and without His love all things are harmful, and act as a veil between man and the Lord of the Kingdom. When His love is there, every bitterness turneth sweet, and every bounty rendereth a wholesome pleasure. For example, a melody, sweet to the ear, bringeth the very spirit of life to a heart in love with God, yet staineth with lust a soul engrossed in sensual desires. And every branch of learning, conjoined with the love of God, is approved and worthy of praise; but bereft of His love, learning is barren—indeed, it bringeth on madness. Every kind of knowledge, every science, is as a tree: if the fruit of it be the love of God, then is it a blessed tree, but if not, that tree is but dried-up wood, and shall only feed the fire.

Selections from the Writings of 'Abdu'l Bahá

O thou son of the Kingdom!

Thy sweet letters with their interesting contents are always conducive to the joy of the hearts. They are like unto the melodies of the nightingale which imparteth exultation to soul and mind. Thank thou God! that thou hast gone to those parts[5] for the purpose of spreading the Word of God and diffusing the holy fragrances of the Kingdom of God and that thou art a gardener in the divine orchard. Ere long, confirmation and assistance shall environ thee.

Tablets of 'Abdu'l-Bahá 'Abbás, vol. 3

---

5   Germany

... this limitless universe is like the human body, all the members of which are connected and linked with one another with the greatest strength. How much the organs, the members and the parts of the body of man are intermingled and connected for mutual aid and help, and how much they influence one another! In the same way, the parts of this infinite universe have their members and elements connected with one another, and influence one another spiritually and materially.

For example, the eye sees, and all the body is affected; the ear hears, and all the members of the body are moved. Of this there is no doubt; and the universe is like a living person. Moreover, the connection which exists between the members of beings must necessarily have an effect and impression, whether it be material or spiritual.

For those who deny spiritual influence upon material things we mention this brief example: wonderful sounds and tones, melodies and charming voices, are accidents which affect the air—for sound is the term for vibrations of the air—and by these vibrations the nerves of the tympanum of the ear are affected, and hearing results. Now reflect that the vibration of the air, which is an accident of no importance, attracts and exhilarates the spirit of man and has great effect upon him: it makes him weep or laugh; perhaps it will influence him to such a degree that he will throw himself into danger. Therefore, see the connection which exists between the spirit of man and the atmospheric vibration, so that the movement of the air becomes the cause of transporting him from one state to another, and of entirely overpowering him; it will deprive him of patience and tranquillity. Consider how strange this is, for nothing comes forth from the singer which enters into the listener; nevertheless, a great spiritual effect is produced. Therefore, surely so great a connection between beings must have spiritual effect and influence.

It has been mentioned that the members and parts of man affect and influence one another. For example, the eye sees; the heart is affected. The ear hears; and the spirit is influenced. The heart is at rest; the thoughts become serene, and for all the members of man's body a pleasant condition is realized. What a connection and what an agreement is this! Since this connection, this spiritual effect and this influence, exists between the members of the body of man, who is only one of many finite beings, certainly between these universal and infinite beings there will also be a spiritual and material connection. Although by existing rules and actual science these connections cannot be discovered, nevertheless, their existence between all beings is certain and absolute.

Some Answered Questions

What a wonderful meeting this is! These are the children of the Kingdom. The song we have just listened to was very beautiful in melody and words. The art of music is divine and effective. It is the food of the soul and spirit. Through the power and charm of music the spirit of man is uplifted. It has wonderful sway and effect in the hearts of children, for their hearts are pure, and melodies have great influence in them. The latent talents with which the hearts of these children are endowed will find expression through the medium of music. Therefore, you must exert yourselves to make them proficient; teach them to sing with excellence and effect. It is incumbent upon each child to know something of music, for without knowledge of this art the melodies of instrument and voice cannot be rightly enjoyed. Likewise, it is necessary that the schools teach it in order that the souls and hearts of the pupils may become vivified and exhilarated and their lives be brightened with enjoyment.

The Promulgation of Universal Peace

My meaning is this, that in every aspect of life, purity and holiness, cleanliness and refinement, exalt the human condition and further the development of man's inner reality. Even in the physical realm, cleanliness will conduce to spirituality, as the Holy Writings clearly state. And although bodily cleanliness is a physical thing, it hath, nevertheless, a powerful influence on the life of the spirit. It is even as a voice wondrously sweet, or a melody played: although sounds are but vibrations in the air which affect the ear's auditory nerve, and these vibrations are but chance phenomena carried along through the air, even so, see how they move the heart. A wondrous melody is wings for the spirit, and maketh the soul to tremble for joy. The purport is that physical cleanliness doth also exert its effect upon the human soul.

Selections from the Writings of 'Abdu'l-Bahá

In the spiritual world the divine bestowals are infinite, for in that realm there is neither separation nor disintegration, which characterize the world of material existence. Spiritual existence is absolute immortality, completeness and unchangeable being. Therefore, we must thank God that He has created for us both material blessings and spiritual bestowals. He has given us material gifts and spiritual graces, outer sight to view the lights of the sun and inner vision by which we may perceive the glory of God. He has designed the outer ear to enjoy the melodies of sound and the inner hearing wherewith we may hear the voice of our Creator. We must strive with energies of heart, soul and mind to develop and manifest the perfections and virtues latent within the realities of the phenomenal world, for the human reality may be compared to a seed. If we sow the seed, a mighty tree appears from it. The virtues of the seed are revealed in the tree; it puts forth branches, leaves, blossoms, and produces fruits. All these virtues were hidden and potential in the seed. Through the blessing and bounty of cultivation these virtues became apparent. Similarly, the merciful God, our Creator, has deposited within human realities certain latent and potential virtues. Through education and culture these virtues deposited by the loving God will become apparent in the human reality, even as the unfoldment of the tree from within the germinating seed. I will pray for you.

The Promulgation of Universal Peace

Through Mirza Ahmad, to the friends and maid-servants of God, Sandusky, Ohio.

Upon them be Baha'o'llah-El-Abha! He is God! O ye who are favored in the Threshold of the Almighty!

Your letter was a rose-garden of significances and from it the fragrance of the Love of God was exhaled. The friends can talk with each other without the lips or tongue, and without the assistance of pen, ink and paper they correspond with each other in the world of heart and spirit. Your brief letter was an indication of those detailed letters. It was the essence of truths and contained innumerable meanings. Therefore, in reality I read in your letter a book, and I felt that all of you are illumined by the light of guidance, are soaring in the infinite sphere of the love of God, like unto the birds singing wonderful melodies in this rose-garden and like unto the nightingale chanting harmonious songs and music. We expect that day after day this melody will become sweeter, this symphony more wonderful and this song more exquisite. It is assured that the confirmations of God will assist that gathering to progress; the boundless gifts will increase and illumine all with the light of guidance.

Upon them be Baha'o'llah-El-Abha!

Star of the West, Bahá'í News, vol. 1, no. 6, 24 June 1910

From the Writings of Shoghi Effendi

Of the exact circumstances attending that epoch-making Declaration we, alas, are but scantily informed. The words Bahá'u'lláh actually uttered on that occasion, the manner of His Declaration, the reaction it produced, its impact on Mírzá Yaḥyá, the identity of those who were privileged to hear Him, are shrouded in an obscurity which future historians will find it difficult to penetrate. The fragmentary description left to posterity by His chronicler Nabíl is one of the very few authentic records we possess of the memorable days He spent in that garden. "Every day," Nabíl has related, "ere the hour of dawn, the gardeners would pick the roses which lined the four avenues of the garden, and would pile them in the center of the floor of His blessed tent. So great would be the heap that when His companions gathered to drink their morning tea in His presence, they would be unable to see each other across it. All these roses Bahá'u'lláh would, with His own hands, entrust to those whom He dismissed from His presence every morning to be delivered, on His behalf, to His Arab and Persian friends in the city." "One night," he continues, "the ninth night of the waxing moon, I happened to be one of those who watched beside His blessed tent. As the hour of midnight approached, I saw Him issue from His tent, pass by the places where some of His companions were sleeping, and begin to pace up and down the moonlit, flower-bordered avenues of the garden. So loud was the singing of the nightingales on every side that only those who were near Him could hear distinctly His voice. He continued to walk until, pausing in the midst of one of these avenues, He observed: 'Consider these nightingales. So great is their love for these roses, that sleepless from dusk till dawn, they warble their melodies and commune with burning passion with the object of their adoration. How then can those who claim to be afire with the rose-like beauty of the Beloved choose to sleep?' For three successive nights I watched and circled round His blessed tent. Every time I passed by the couch whereon He lay, I would find Him wakeful, and every day, from morn till eventide, I would see Him ceaselessly engaged in conversing with the stream of visitors who kept flowing in from Baghdád. Not once could I discover in the words He spoke any trace of dissimulation."

God Passes By

The executioners, though accustomed to their own gruesome task, would themselves be amazed at the fiendish cruelty of the populace. Women and children could be seen led down the streets by their executioners, their flesh in ribbons, with candles burning in their wounds, singing with ringing voices before the silent spectators: "Verily from God we come, and unto Him we return!"

God Passes By

As regard the chanting of Tablets in the Temple, Shoghi Effendi wishes in this connection to urge the friends to avoid all forms of rigidity and uniformity in matters of worship. There is no objection to the recital or chanting of prayers in the Oriental language, but there is also no obligation whatsoever of adopting such a form of prayer at any devotional service in the auditorium of the Temple. It should neither be required nor prohibited. The important thing that should always be borne in mind is that with the exception of certain specific obligatory prayers, Bahá'u'lláh has given us no strict or special rulings in matters of worship, whether in the Temple or else-where. Prayer is essentially a communion between man and God, and as such transcends all ritualistic forms and formulae.

Directives from the Guardian

One night, aware that the hour of her death was at hand, she[6] put on the attire of a bride, and annointed herself with perfume, and, sending for the wife of the Kalantar, she communicated to her the secret of her impending martyrdom, and confided to her her last wishes. Then, closeting herself in her chambers, she awaited, in prayer and meditation, the hour which was to witness her reunion with her Beloved. She was pacing the floor of her room, chanting a litany expressive of both grief and triumph, when the farráshes of Azíz Khán-i-Sardár arrived, in the dead of night, to conduct her to the Ílkhání garden, which lay beyond the city gates, and which was to be the site of her martyrdom.

God Passes By

The cup of Bahá'u'lláh's sorrows was now running over. All His exhortations, all His efforts to remedy a rapidly deteriorating situation, had remained fruitless. The velocity of His manifold woes was hourly and visibly increasing. Upon the sadness that filled His soul and the gravity of the situation confronting Him, His writings, revealed during that somber period, throw abundant light. In some of His prayers He poignantly confesses that "tribulation upon tribulation" had gathered about Him, that "adversaries with one consent" had fallen upon Him, that "wretchedness" had grievously touched Him, and that "woes at their blackest" had befallen Him. God Himself He calls upon as a Witness to His "sighs and lamentations," His "powerlessness, poverty and destitution," to the "injuries" He sustained, and the "abasement" He suffered. "So grievous hath been My weeping," He, in one of these prayers, avows, "that I have been prevented from making mention of Thee and singing Thy praises."

God Passes By

---

6 Tahirih

'Abdu'l-Bahá has written that "Among certain nations of the East, music was considered reprehensible". Though the Qur'án contains no specific guidance on the subject, some Muslims consider listening to music as unlawful, while others tolerate music within certain bounds and subject to particular conditions.

There are a number of passages in the Bahá'í Writings in praise of music. 'Abdu'l-Bahá, for example, asserts that "music, sung or played, is spiritual food for soul and heart".

Kitáb-i-Aqdas

How many a night did she[7] whom the world wronged spend as a prisoner, worn with care, tormented, banished from her home. How many a day did she live through as an exile and a captive! There was no venom of affliction, at the hands of this Faith's foes, that was not given her to drink, no arrow of cruelty but struck her holy breast. Yet in spite of the endless tribulations and disasters, she who was a spirit of holiness and a songster of Heaven, would even in the midst of dire ordeals, her face aglow, bloom like a rose.

Cited in Bahíyyih Khánum, the Greatest Holy Leaf, p. 82.

From the Universal House of Justice

We recall the testimony of His distinguished sister, the Greatest Holy Leaf, that "in the dark of the night, out of the depths of His bosom, could be heard His burning sighs, and when the day broke, the wondrous music of His prayers would rise up to the denizens of the realm on high."

27 November 2021

---

7   Greatest Holy Leaf

MELODIES IN THE
MASHRIQU'L-ADHKÁR

From the Writings of Bahá'u'lláh

Teach your children the verses revealed from the heaven of majesty and power, so that, in most melodious tones, they may recite the Tablets of the All-Merciful in the alcoves within the Mashriqu'l-Adhkárs. Whoever hath been transported by the rapture born of adoration for My Name, the Most Compassionate, will recite the verses of God in such wise as to captivate the hearts of those yet wrapped in slumber. Well is it with him who hath quaffed the Mystic Wine of everlasting life from the utterance of his merciful Lord in My Name—a Name through which every lofty and majestic mountain hath been reduced to dust.

Kitáb-i-Aqdas

From the Writings of 'Abdu'l-Bahá

O Lord, our God! We are helpless; Thou art the Lord of strength and power. We are wretched; Thou art the Almighty, the All-Glorious. We are poor; Thou art the All-Possessing, the Most Generous. Graciously assist us in our servitude to Thy sacred Threshold, and aid us, through Thy strengthening grace, to worship Thee at the dawning-places of Thy praise. Enable us to diffuse Thy holy fragrances amongst Thy creatures, and strengthen our loins to serve Thee amidst Thy servants, so that we may guide all nations to Thy Most Great Name and lead all peoples to the shores of the glorious ocean of Thy oneness.

O Lord! Deliver us from the attachments of the world and its peoples, from the transgressions of the past, and from the afflictions yet to come, that we may arise to exalt Thy Word with the utmost joy and radiance and celebrate Thy praise in the daytime and in the night season, that we may summon all people to the way of guidance and enjoin them to observe righteousness, and that we may chant the verses of Thy unity amidst all Thy creation. Potent art Thou to do what pleaseth Thee. Thou art, verily, the Almighty, the Most Powerful.

Twenty-six Prayers Revealed by 'Abdu'l-Bahá

In the organization of the Mashrak-el-Azcar, thou art indeed well striving. I hope thou wilt attain a great reward, open an eloquent tongue, raise a wonderful melody in every meeting, draw and paint the images and forms of the Kingdom in the material world.

Rest assured in the grace of the Lord and be dilated by His infinite favors.

Tablets of 'Abdu'l-Bahá 'Abbás, vol. 2

The utmost joy was attained, for—praise be to God! —the friends of the Merciful passed some time on that day joyous and singing in the land of the Mashrak-el-Azcar and enjoyed commemorating the Lord of the verses with the greatest joy. That melody was heard by the Supreme Concourse and that rose-song of the nightingale of faithfulness gladdened the people of the rose-garden of ABHA.

I am hopeful that, during the coming Rizwan,[1] a great feast shall be held in the land of the Mashrak-el-Azcar, a spiritual celebration prepared and the melodies of the violin and the mandoline and hymns in praise and glorification of the Lord of Hosts make all the audience joyous and ecstatic.

Tablets of 'Abdu'l-Bahá 'Abbás, vol. 1

O thou who art attracted by the Fragrances of God!

Verily, I chanted thy poem. Its significance was beautiful, its composition eloquent and its words excellent. It was like the melody of the birds of holiness in the paradise of El-ABHA. The breasts of the maid-servants of the Merciful were exhilarated by its chanting. Blessed art thou for uttering forth such an excellent poem and brilliant pearl.

Verily, these verses shall be sung in the divine meetings and in the assemblages of the spiritual in the course of ages and centuries to come, for thou hast uttered the praise of thy Lord and expressed significant meanings in eulogy of thy Lord, the Merciful, the Clement. All poems shall be forgotten in the course of time save those that are extraordinary; thy poem shall be chanted with melody and best voices in the Center of Worship (or Mashrak-el-Azcar) forevermore.

Tablets of 'Abdu'l-Bahá 'Abbás, vol. 1

---

1   21 April, 1909

Temples are symbols of the reality and divinity of God—the collective center of mankind. Consider how within a temple every race and people is seen and represented—all in the presence of the Lord, covenanting together in a covenant of love and fellowship, all offering the same melody, prayer and supplication to God. Therefore, it is evident that the church is a collective center for mankind. For this reason there have been churches and temples in all the divine religions; but the real Collective Centers are the Manifestations of God, of Whom the church or temple is a symbol and expression. That is to say, the Manifestation of God is the real divine temple and Collective Center of which the outer church is but a symbol.

The Promulgation of Universal Peace

It befitteth the friends to hold a gathering, a meeting, where they shall glorify God and fix their hearts upon Him, and read and recite the Holy Writings of the Blessed Beauty—may my soul be the ransom of His lovers! The lights of the All-Glorious Realm, the rays of the Supreme Horizon, will be cast upon such bright assemblages, for these are none other than the Mashriqu'l-Adhkárs, the Dawning-Points of God's Remembrance, which must, at the direction of the Most Exalted Pen, be established in every hamlet and city ... These spiritual gatherings must be held with the utmost purity and consecration, so that from the site itself, and its earth and the air about it, one will inhale the fragrant breathings of the Holy Spirit.

Selections from the Writings of 'Abdu'l-Bahá

Truly, pure and radiant hearts are the dawning-places of the mention of God from which the melodies of supplication and prayer continually reach the Concourse on high.

The Institution of the Mashriqu'l-Adhkár (compilation)

The Ma<u>sh</u>riqu'l-A<u>dh</u>kár is the dawning-place of lights and the gathering place of the righteous. Whenever a company of noble souls assemble in a heavenly gathering there and offer supplications, intone divine verses, and chant prayers with wondrous melodies, the inmates of the Concourse on high hearken and call out, crying, "Happy are we; let all the world rejoice!" for, praise be unto God, souls from among the angels of the Kingdom of Glory have arisen in the nether world to commune with their Lord and intone the verses of Divine Unity in a gathering of holiness. What bounty is there greater than this?

The Institution of the Ma<u>sh</u>riqu'l-A<u>dh</u>kár (compilation)

The Ma<u>sh</u>riqu'l-A<u>dh</u>kár is a divine edifice in this nether world and a means for attaining the oneness of humanity, inasmuch as all the peoples of the world shall gather in fellowship and harmony within the Ma<u>sh</u>riqu'l-A<u>dh</u>kár and, chanting the anthems of Divine Unity, engage in the praise and glorification of the Lord of Hosts. Thy joy must, of a certainty, rest in diffusing the light of divine guidance.

The Institution of the Ma<u>sh</u>riqu'l-A<u>dh</u>kár (compilation)

When the Ma<u>sh</u>riqu'l-A<u>dh</u>kár is completed, when the lights are emanating therefrom, and the righteous assemble therein, when prayers are offered to the Kingdom of divine mysteries and the voice of glorification is raised to the Supreme Lord, then shall the believers rejoice, and their hearts be dilated, overflowing with the love of the ever-living and self-subsisting God.

The Institution of the Ma<u>sh</u>riqu'l-A<u>dh</u>kár (compilation)

O ye loved ones of God! The news was received that a Mashriqu'l-Adhkár hath been established, that in that land the praise and glorification of God hath reached the Kingdom of Glory and the melodies of worship and praise of that glorious Beloved have ascended to the Concourse on high. What boundless joy and delight were produced by these glad-tidings ...

The Institution of the Mashriqu'l-Adhkár (compilation)

From the Writings of Shoghi Effendi

It should be borne in mind that the central Edifice of the Mashriqu'l-Adhkár, round which in the fullness of time shall cluster such institutions of social service as shall afford relief to the suffering, sustenance to the poor, shelter to the wayfarer, solace to the bereaved, and education to the ignorant, should be regarded, apart from these Dependencies, as a House solely designed and entirely dedicated to the worship of God ...

25 October 1929, Bahá'í Administration

And thus having recognized in Bahá'u'lláh the Source whence this celestial light proceeds, they will irresistibly feel attracted to seek the shelter of His House, and congregate therein, unhampered by ceremonials and unfettered by creed, to render homage to the one true God, the Essence and Orb of eternal Truth, and to exalt and magnify the name of His Messengers and Prophets Who, from time immemorial even unto our day, have, under divers circumstances and in varying measure, mirrored forth to a dark and wayward world the light of heavenly Guidance.

25 October 1929, Bahá'í Administration

EFFORT TO DIFFUSE
DIVINE MELODIES

From the Writings of Bahá'u'lláh

Not every sea hath pearls; not every branch will flower, nor will the nightingale sing thereon. Then, ere the nightingale of the mystic Paradise repair to the celestial garden, and the rays of the morn of inner meaning return to the Day-Star of Truth, make thou an effort, that haply in this dust-heap of a mortal world thou mayest catch a fragrance from the everlasting rose-garden and live in the shadow of the inhabitants of this everlasting city. And when thou hast attained this highest plane and most exalted degree, then shalt thou gaze on the Beloved and forget all else.

The Call of the Divine Beloved

O people of Bahá! The source of crafts, sciences and arts is the power of reflection. Make ye every effort that out of this ideal mine there may gleam forth such pearls of wisdom and utterance as will promote the well-being and harmony of all the kindreds of the earth.

Tablets of Bahá'u'lláh Revealed After the Kitáb-i-Aqdas

O peoples of the world! Forsake all evil, hold fast that which is good. Strive to be shining examples unto all mankind, and true reminders of the virtues of God amidst men. He that riseth to serve My Cause should manifest My wisdom, and bend every effort to banish ignorance from the earth. Be united in counsel, be one in thought. Let each morn be better than its eve and each morrow richer than its yesterday. Man's merit lieth in service and virtue and not in the pageantry of wealth and riches. Take heed that your words be purged from idle fancies and worldly desires and your deeds be cleansed from craftiness and suspicion. Dissipate not the wealth of your precious lives in the pursuit of evil and corrupt affection, nor let your endeavours be spent in promoting your personal interest. Be generous in your days of plenty, and be patient in the hour of loss. Adversity is followed by success and rejoicings follow woe. Guard against idleness and sloth, and cling unto that which profiteth mankind, whether young or old, whether high or low. Beware lest ye sow tares of dissension among men or plant thorns of doubt in pure and radiant hearts.

Tablets of Bahá'u'lláh Revealed After the Kitáb-i-Aqdas

From the exalted source, and out of the essence of His favor and bounty He hath entrusted every created thing with a sign of His knowledge, so that none of His creatures may be deprived of its share in expressing, each according to its capacity and rank, this knowledge. This sign is the mirror of His beauty in the world of creation. The greater the effort exerted for the refinement of this sublime and noble mirror, the more faithfully will it be made to reflect the glory of the names and attributes of God, and reveal the wonders of His signs and knowledge. Every created thing will be enabled (so great is this reflecting power) to reveal the potentialities of its pre-ordained station, will recognize its capacity and limitations, and will testify to the truth that "He, verily, is God; there is none other God besides Him." ...

There can be no doubt whatever that, in consequence of the efforts which every man may consciously exert and as a result of the exertion of his own spiritual faculties, this mirror can be so cleansed from the dross of earthly defilements and purged from satanic fancies as to be able to draw nigh unto the meads of eternal holiness and attain the courts of everlasting fellowship.
Gleanings from the Writings of Bahá'u'lláh

Make thou an effort, that haply thou mayest obtain the afore-mentioned Tablets and acquire therefrom a share of the pearls of wisdom and utterance that have issued from the treasury of the Pen of the All-Merciful. The glory of God rest upon thee, upon every steadfast and unwavering heart and upon every constant and faithful soul.
The Tabernacle of Unity

From the Writings of 'Abdu'l-Bahá

Consequently, the believers of God must display the utmost effort, upraise the divine melody throughout those regions, promulgate the heavenly teachings and waft over all the spirit of eternal life, so that those republics may become so illumined with the splendors and the effulgences of the Sun of Reality that they may become the objects of the praise and commendation of all other countries ... the intention must be purified, the effort ennobled and exalted, so that you may establish affinity between the hearts of the world of humanity. This glorious aim will not become realized save through the promotion of divine teachings which are the foundations of the holy religions.
Tablets of the Divine Plan

O thou servant of the Beauty of Abha!

We considered all that thou hast written. It seems that the maid-servant of God, Mrs ... hath arisen to deliver (the truth). If she advanceth in this manner, maketh more effort and day by day groweth in spirituality, sincerity, devotion and severance, in a short time she will become purely merciful and will spiritualize others; she will progress in the stations of sanctity and purity; she will become the possessor of a fluent speech and will find her heart brilliant and full of serenity and faith to such an extent that her pure breath will so take effect even in stone, tree and clay (i.e., in all people), that she, herself, will be astonished. When the interior parts of musical instruments become clear and polished, their tone will take effect and warm the hearts. I hope the maid-servant of God, Mrs ... may attain to this degree, for she is capable.

Tablets of 'Abdu'l-Bahá 'Abbás, vol 3

O thou sign of the Kingdom and the bird singing with the most wonderful melodies in the rose-garden of Paradise! ...

O thou maid-servant of God! Display thou an effort, gird up the loins of endeavor, dilate thy breast and be thou prepared for the manifestation of the breaths of the Holy Spirit in thine heart. By God, the true One, verily, the Holy Spirit confirmeth every maid-servant who ariseth to spread the fragrances of God, so that the inhabitants of the whole world cannot overcome her spiritual strength—for similar things have happened in the past centuries.

Tablets of 'Abdu'l-Bahá 'Abbás, vol. 3

I hope that you may become assisted and confirmed, and never lose courage in the promotion of the divine teachings. Day by day may you add to your effort, exertion, and magnanimity.

Tablets of the Divine Plan

Thou hast written concerning the tests that have come upon thee. To the sincere ones, tests are as a gift from God, the Exalted, for a heroic person hasteneth, with the utmost joy and gladness, to the tests of a violent battlefield, but the coward is afraid and trembles and utters moaning and lamentation. Likewise, an expert student prepareth and memorizeth his lessons and exercises with the utmost effort, and in the day of examination he appeareth with infinite joy before the master. Likewise, the pure gold shineth radiantly in the fire of test. Consequently, it is made clear that for holy souls, trials are as the gift of God, the Exalted; but for weak souls they are an unexpected calamity. This test is just as thou hast written: it removeth the rust of egotism from the mirror of the heart until the Sun of Truth may shine therein. For, no veil is greater than egotism and no matter how thin that covering may be, yet it will finally veil man entirely and prevent him from receiving a portion from the eternal bounty.

Tablets of ʿAbduʾl-Bahá ʿAbbás, vol. 3

In brief, I hope you will display in this respect the greatest effort and magnanimity. It is assured that you will become assisted and confirmed. A person declaring the glad tidings of the appearance of the realities and significances of the Kingdom is like unto a farmer who scatters pure seeds in the rich soil. The spring cloud will pour upon them the rain of bounty, and unquestionably the station of the farmer will be raised in the estimation of the lord of the village, and many harvests will be gathered.

Therefore, ye friends of God! Appreciate ye the value of this time and be ye engaged in the sowing of the seeds, so that you may find the heavenly blessing and the lordly bestowal. Upon you be Baháʾuʾl-Abhá!

Tablets of the Divine Plan

O ye friends of God! Be kind to all peoples and nations, have love for all of them, exert yourselves to purify the hearts as much as you can, and bestow abundant effort in rejoicing the souls ... Exert with your soul; seek no rest in body; supplicate and beseech with your heart and search for divine assistance and favor, in order that ye may make this world the Paradise of ABHA and this terrestrial globe the arena of the Supreme Kingdom. If ye make an effort, it is certain that these lights will shine, this cloud of mercy shall rain, this soul-nourishing breeze shall waft, and the scent of this most fragrant musk be diffused.

Tablets of ʿAbduʾl-Bahá ʿAbbás, vol. 1

It is incumbent upon thee to make thy greatest effort; to put forth thy full strength; to supplicate and to worship, and to be careful to put thy full trust in the Kingdom of the Lord Most High.

Tablets of ʿAbduʾl-Bahá ʿAbbás, vol. 2

Make thou an effort that thou mayest take thy place under the sun and receive an abundant share of its dazzling light.

Selections from the Writings of ʿAbduʾl-Bahá

It is, therefore, evident and proved that an effort must be put forward to complete the purpose and plan of the teachings of God in order that in this great Day of days the world may be reformed, souls resuscitated, a new spirit of life found, hearts become illumined, mankind rescued from the bondage of nature, saved from the baseness of materialism and attain spirituality and radiance in attraction toward the divine Kingdom. This is necessary; this is needful. Mere reading of the Holy Books and texts will not suffice.

The Promulgation of Universal Peace

If only ye exert the effort, it is certain that these splendours will shine out, these clouds of mercy will shed down their rain, these life-giving winds will rise and blow, this sweet-smelling musk will be scattered far and wide.

Selections from the Writings of 'Abdu'l-Bahá

Consequently, if one looks for praiseworthy results and wishes to produce eternal effects, let him make exceeding effort, in order that Green Acre may become an assemblage for the Word of God and a gathering place for the spiritual ones of the heavenly world.

Tablets of 'Abdu'l-Bahá 'Abbás, vol. 2

As to you: Your efforts must be lofty. Exert yourselves with heart and soul so that, perchance, through your efforts the light of universal peace may shine and this darkness of estrangement and enmity may be dispelled from amongst men, that all men may become as one family and consort together in love and kindness, that the East may assist the West and the West give help to the East, for all are the inhabitants of one planet, the people of one original native land and the flocks of one Shepherd.

The Promulgation of Universal Peace

O ye believers of God! Exalt your effort and magnify your aims.

Tablets of the Divine Plan

For a man who has love, effort is a rest.

'Abdu'l-Bahá in London

Question: One of the powers possessed by the Divine Manifestations is knowledge. To what extent is it limited?

Answer: Knowledge is of two kinds. One is subjective and the other objective knowledge—that is to say, an intuitive knowledge and a knowledge derived from perception.

The knowledge of things which men universally have is gained by reflection or by evidence—that is to say, either by the power of the mind the conception of an object is formed, or from beholding an object the form is produced in the mirror of the heart. The circle of this knowledge is very limited because it depends upon effort and attainment. But the second sort of knowledge, which is the knowledge of being, is intuitive; it is like the cognizance and consciousness that man has of himself.

For example, the mind and the spirit of man are cognizant of the conditions and states of the members and component parts of the body, and are aware of all the physical sensations; in the same way, they are aware of their power, of their feelings, and of their spiritual conditions. This is the knowledge of being which man realizes and perceives, for the spirit surrounds the body and is aware of its sensations and powers. This knowledge is not the outcome of effort and study. It is an existing thing; it is an absolute gift.

Some Answered Questions

It is from the bounty of God that man is selected for the highest degree; and the differences which exist between men in regard to spiritual progress and heavenly perfections are also due to the choice of the Compassionate One ... Nevertheless, by effort and perseverance, knowledge, science and other perfections can be acquired; but only the light of the Divine Beauty can transport and move the spirits through the force of attraction.

Some Answered Questions

O ye real friends! Make ye an effort that this universe may become another universe and this darkened world find a ray of the Sun of Truth and become luminous and refulgent.

Tablets of 'Abdu'l-Bahá 'Abbás, vol. 3

If ye make an effort, it is certain that these lights will shine, this cloud of mercy shall rain, this soul-nourishing breeze shall waft, and the scent of this most fragrant musk be diffused.

Tablets of 'Abdu'l-Bahá 'Abbás, vol. 1

Seize the opportunity, use every effort and depend not upon circumstances which produce no fruits. Spend thy days, with all joy and fragrance, in speaking to the praise of God, being gladdened through His good tidings, in rejoicing through His graces and in spreading His breaths.

Tablets of 'Abdu'l-Bahá 'Abbás, vol. 3

Effort, the utmost effort, is required. Should you display an effort, so that the fragrances of God may be diffused among the Eskimos, its effect will be very great and far-reaching. God says in the great Qur'án: A day will come wherein the lights of unity will enlighten all the world.

Tablets of the Divine Plan

I rejoice to hear that thou takest pains with thine art, for in this wonderful new age, art is worship. The more thou strivest to perfect it, the closer wilt thou come to God. What bestowal could be greater than this, that one's art should be even as the act of worshipping the Lord?

Additional Tablets, Extracts and Talks

"The day will come when
the Cause will spread like wildfire
when its spirit and teachings
will be presented on the stage or
in art and literature as a whole.

Art can better awaken such noble
sentiments than cold rationalizing,
especially among the mass of the people."

Universal House of Justice, 21 April 1996.